COMMUNICATE FOR A CHANGE

"COMMUNICATE FOR A CHANGE,,

REVITALIZING CONVERSATIONS
FOR
HIGHER EDUCATION

Lori Carrell & Robert Zemsky

 JOHNS HOPKINS UNIVERSITY PRESS | *Baltimore*

Johns Hopkins University Press
2715 North Charles Street
Baltimore, Maryland 21218-4363
www.press.jhu.edu

Library of Congress Cataloging-in-Publication Data

Names: Carrell, Lori, 1962– author. | Zemsky, Robert, 1940– author.
Title: Communicate for a change : revitalizing conversations for higher
    education / Lori Carrell and Robert Zemsky.
Description: Baltimore : Johns Hopkins University Press, 2021. | Includes
    bibliographical references and index.
Identifiers: LCCN 2020048882 | ISBN 9781421441740 (hardcover) | ISBN
    9781421441757 (ebook)
Subjects: LCSH: Education, Higher—Aims and objectives—United States. |
    College teachers—Professional relationships—United States. |
    Communication in education—United States. | Educational change—United
    States.
Classification: LCC LA227.4 .C368 2021 | DDC 378.73—dc23
LC record available at https://lccn.loc.gov/2020048882

A catalog record for this book is available from the British Library.

*Special discounts are available for bulk purchases of this book. For more information,
please contact Special Sales at specialsales@jh.edu.*

Johns Hopkins University Press uses environmentally friendly book materials,
including recycled text paper that is composed of at least 30 percent post-consumer
waste, whenever possible.

For our children and our children's children.
It is their futures that motivate us.

CONTENTS

We clearly believe in group work: group conversations, group adventures, group books. Accordingly, our debts to our friends, colleagues, and students loom large. We need to first thank our conversation partners, whose contributions made this book richer and whose comments and suggestions made it better. Here again, in the order in which they appear in the text, are those whose contributions made our task not just easier but more fun: Susan Campbell Baldridge, coauthor of *The College Stress Test* and former provost of Middlebury College; Teri Pipe, chief well-being officer, Arizona State University; Joan T. A. Gabel, president, University of Minnesota; Randall Bass, vice president for strategic education initiatives, Georgetown University; Lynn Pasquerella, president, Association of American Colleges and Universities; William Massy, former chief financial officer and professor emeritus, Stanford University; Cheyenne Carrell, Prescott College alum; Nevaeh Nez, University of Minnesota Rochester sophomore; Mark Putnam, president, Central College; Freeman A. Hrabowski, president, University of Maryland Baltimore County (UMBC); Peter H. Henderson, senior advisor, Office of the President, and policy fellow, School of Public Policy, UMBC; and J. Kathleen Tracy, associate professor, School of Medicine, University of Maryland, and ACE Fellow at UMBC.

We also benefited from the efforts of those who closely read the manuscript while it was in draft: First, Greg Wegner, who has been an editorial shepherd for much of our work. Ann Duffield helped us position our work amidst all those who focus on the best strategies for effective communication. Linda Oubre helped us think through a workable strategy for the conversation on differences. Franca Barricelli affirmed core concepts and topics. And, of course, our spouses, with whom we're grateful to engage in lifelong, sustaining conversations.

As before, Greg Britton of Johns Hopkins University Press was the godfather we needed. Truly, he gave us the courage of our convictions.

COMMUNICATE FOR A CHANGE

Let's Talk

What you have before you is a very different kind of book, one that is about having the conversations higher education regularly avoids. Ours is also a book written by talkers who believe in conversation for its own sake. We understand well the hubris that underlies this project. Put simply, we want our conversation to promote change led from within rather than imposed from without the academy.

We have been having these conversations with each other and with colleagues and friends for nearly a decade now. In the process we've come to understand exactly what it is that we have in common. We're primarily teachers who love teaching, and though we're from different disciplinary traditions, we share a pair of commitments defining our scholarship. The first is the necessity of securing good data on which to base decision making. An even more compelling commonality motivating our friendship is a fascination with conversation itself. Each of us knows that securing a better future requires talking openly, frankly, and honestly about the academy we seek. That is what productive as well as safe conversations entail.

Just as important, we understand our differences. One of us elicits candor and trust by paying attention to what others have to say. The other is a provocateur whose arguments push people. We both know how to listen carefully. Lori is the optimist, sure that our collective genius and redemptive purpose in higher education holds out the promise of igniting ideas that will change the world for the better. She entered academia with a firmly held conviction that every spoken word has the potential for permanent impact. Her mentor was Francis E. X. Dance, professor extraordinaire in a University of Denver PhD program focused on human communication and its interaction with thought. What makes it all work are the conversations with colleagues who use evidence to generate and then implement good ideas. What she sought from the get-go were colleagues whose way of being stimulates her own thinking and inspires action. Bob is the cynic among us, often reminded by the University of Pennsylvania's Martin Meyerson that it would be a good idea to temper his fondness for end-of-the-world pronouncements. Where Lori's scholarship focuses first on language and expression, Bob's work most often begins with an exploration of the patterns within the data.

About a year ago we began a new round of storytelling. We reviewed the projects that we shared in the past to see if the lessons we drew from those experiences are still relevant today (for the most part they are), but like most denizens of the academy we have been dismayed by how sharp the cultural and political divides within our communities have become. We needed to look each other in the eye to make sure each of us, though in different ways, understood that learning is the necessary ingredient for meaningful change in higher education.

At the outset we joked that we were engaged in an endeavor only Gilbert and Sullivan would have understood—and they had the advantage of split responsibilities; Gilbert wrote the words, Sullivan composed the music. We, however, were to be jointly responsible for each of the conversations we wanted to initiate. More than that, we would have to jointly decide which stories to hang our hats on, though we conceded early on that each story could teach a multitude of lessons.

What saved us was the discovery that we had the same kind of conversations in mind. Conversations, to our way of thinking, are not negotiations, though good conversation can set the stage for the deliberative process on which a shared consensus ultimately depends. While it is possible, even productive, to agree on a common starting point for such a conversation, agreeing in advance as to how the conversation is to conclude robs the exchange of its spontaneity. Agendas are out, as are declarations and pronouncements. In good conversation there are no victors, just participants— or as we are wont to say, just good learners ready to consider alternatives. It is important to trust the process and let the exchange of ideas and stories take a conversation where it needs to go.

To get the process started we did in fact have to play Gilbert and Sullivan, who each time they set out to write a new opera would first need to agree upon a setting, whether it be a ship or mysterious Japan or the idiocies of the British judicial system. More prosaically, the challenge we set for ourselves was to identify a list of truly critical topics worthy of the kind of conversations we had in mind. That took us some time and consultation, but eventually we settled on the list of topics embedded in our table of contents.

Next we had to invent a way to model a good conversation focusing separately on each of our chosen topics. After considerable experimentation we came up with what we call a "serve-and-volley" methodology. We begin each conversation with one of us serving up the topic by writing a brief "opening shot" that sets the conversation's context. Then the other starts the volley. Ultimately, with this style we seek to demonstrate our premise about the transformative potential of conversation—a sharp contrast to the traditional approach that situates authors as solitary knowledge disseminators.

One last insight shaped how we proceeded. We could not be the only contributors. We would need to test our interactions with a diverse collection of colleagues. So, we invited expert practitioners and change agents to add their voices to our conversations. They became our conversation partners. Their perspectives ensure we are not just talking to ourselves, oblivious to new communication realities or lived experiences that differ dramatically from our own. We are immensely grateful for those who accepted our invitation.

Each of our conversations engage the academy in a subject that has proved truly difficult to navigate. Each stands alone, though some ideas broached in one conversation inevitably spill over into subsequent conversations. What we have produced are actual starting conversations to serve as catalysts that we hope will kick-start subsequent deliberations. The courage and stamina to convene these conversations requires an understanding of just how much what we have in mind is a radical departure from the norms across higher education. While many insights and good ideas will likely emerge, the goal of these conversations is not to produce a white paper or some kind of reform proposal by a specific date. Instead, the aim is to foster genuine talk about issues that matter, strengthening trust and agency. The attitude of the participants toward the value of their work may change, impacting their well-being. New relationships may be formed, enhancing the quality of campus life. And, through these conversations, fresh perspectives for revolutionary change may occur.

Conversation One. Why Can't We Talk about the Mess We're In?

We want to tackle first the sense of disparagement now too often characteristic of the academy. The question we want everyone to ask is: Why can't we talk about the mess we're in? Asking that question leads almost directly to a spiraling set of related ruminations. Why is there so little good news? Why has it proved so easy to cut public funding for higher education, all the while portraying colleges and universities as places of waste and extravagance? Why is the list of scandals seemingly endless? Sexual harassment. Declining enrollments. Leaders driven from office. The overriding question embedded in this litany is simply: How can the academy talk about its declining sense of itself without, on the one hand, giving succor to hostile critics, and, on the other, burying its head in the sand?

Conversation Two. Will a Commitment to Community Actually Move Us Forward?

Our second conversation asks a more deliberative question: "Will a commitment to community actually move us forward?" We understand that simply celebrating the virtues of community is not an answer. Can higher education actually talk about how and why community matters in such a way as to collectively commit to a changed reality? What systemic rules would need to be broken to move in such a direction? Building genuine community requires meaningful conversation, and that requires vulnerability, mutual and authentic feedback, and the routine of an ongoing willingness to adapt. We wondered if presidents need to be more intentional in their facilitation of community-generating dialogue, and ultimately we asked, "Can higher education embrace a notion of collective well-being that is neither trivial nor simply saccharine?"

Conversation Three. The Slogans That Ensnare Us

Our third conversation shifts the focus to the academy's increasingly dysfunctional arguments over campus governance. Here we start in search of a campuswide conversation that examines "the slogans that ensnare us"—academic freedom, workforce, equity and inclusion, and more. Why do these terms so often become triggers or weapons rather than means to agreed-upon ends? If the academy is full of the kind of smart people we know them to be, why do we trip on polarizing words like everyone else? Might we instead search for a language of authority and accountability as well as inclusion and equity that serves as a unifying catalyst for transformation?

Conversation Four. Why Can't We Connect with Each Other?

The next requisite conversation asks: "Why can't we connect with each other?" What must transpire before campuses deal with the conditions that disconnect people and ideas? Instead of defaulting to "silo" language, an accepted part of academic culture, the transformation we seek needs to promote meaningful connections across disciplinary divides among us all—students, faculty, staff, administrators, industry partners, generations, and even external higher ed skeptics. If faculty are to lead change from within, regardless of their level of introversion, they cannot continue to expect to be independent contractors. And what about disconnected ideas? If we truly seek revitalization in higher education, our research and teaching missions must be much more intentionally intertwined. Here the conversation we seek must unabashedly promote the one kind of connective tissue we all share: a commitment to learning.

Conversation Five. Why Are We the Bad Guys?

Equally perplexing has been the increasingly dismal portrayal of higher education in general and of the faculty in particular. Our fifth conversation asks: "Why are we the bad guys?" Too often faculty are being presented as self-centered occupants of institutions that have lost touch with those they are expected to serve and protect. The cruelest charge is that the faculty act as if the academy's traditional commitment to free speech is a shield against the public's efforts to hold the academy accountable. Any countering discussion will first have to sort the wheat from the chaff by asking, "To what extent does combating this negative portrayal require changed behaviors as well?"

Conversation Six. Money Talks

The next necessary conversation involves a simple but all-too-true observation: "Money talks." The problem is that relatively few within the academy and even fewer within the faculty know how to talk about money. The easy assumption that it's all about "butts in seats" is simply false. Collegiate economies are complex blends of basic truths (there is no free lunch) and a host of processes and traditions designed to limit options. What is also clear is that higher education has a history of talking about rather than achieving change, almost always blaming the lack of sufficient resources.

Conversation Seven. The Students We Hardly Know

It's time to talk frankly about the fact that our students are increasingly different from us, the faculty who teach them. They are in fact, "the students we hardly know." Among other phenomena we need to take account of is an awareness of the historical and cultural contexts in which young minds have been developing. Most of us in the privileged role of teacher were not digital natives and did not grow up with active shooter drills, nor did we come of age with the rates of depression and anxiety that today's young people experience. There is plenty of glib talk about generational differences without a corresponding deep dialogue about how those differences might serve as a catalyst for different kinds of curricula and learning experiences. A growing literature in neuroscience and beyond ought to compel us to pay attention and make adjustments. Here, listening to the learners themselves is itself an imperative.

Conversation Eight. Is It Ever Safe to Talk about Changing the Curriculum?

Our eighth conversation asks: "Is it ever safe to talk about changing the curriculum?" Focusing on the curriculum touches one of the most perilous of the academy's third rails. For many in higher ed, vocationalism is dismissed out-of-hand. Being educated means first and foremost being educated in the liberal arts. Competency-based education is viewed with suspicion, as too deep a bow to "training" instead of true education. The disciplines are presented as immutable elements of an academic periodic table that can be added to but not subtracted from. And the processes for enacting curricular change? Well, let's just say for now that those processes do not move at the same speed as the accelerated pace of change outside the academy. What is also clear is that the curriculum remains the provenance of the faculty. We are in charge and ought to remain so. As in the case of the discussion of money, what is required is a set of well-thought-out curricular proposals that have been fully vetted with all constituencies. The faculty can propose, but only the campus writ large can dispose—and that will require a process for first considering and then enacting alternative curricula.

Conversation Nine. Why Can't We Have a Productive Conversation about Race and Gender?

What we have before us is a catalog of the tough questions higher education has largely left unaddressed: disparagement, communitas, weaponized words, the connect-disconnect conundrum, money, faculty as villains, unknown student perspectives, and our often untouchable curriculum. One more. Here we come to the most disruptive of the conversations higher education has not convened, at least not in a way that has led to systemic change. The truth of the matter is that higher education, like most of the nation, needs to ask: "Why can't we have a productive conversation about race and gender?" Instead of having such discussions, the academy makes speeches, declarations, pronouncements, and, more often than not, experiences long, awkward silences. Those who aren't angry are afraid, having determined that it is safest to say nothing at all. The fundamental issues go unresolved, because they are not addressed. Talking about race and gender is not easy, but such talk is necessary, especially now. There is also an underlying tension between two strategies for moving forward. One builds on the assumption we are being held hostage by an antipathy to cultural confrontation that must be addressed directly. The alternative strategy calls for more practical, specific problem-solving conversations that by design hold space for emotion while focusing on action.

Reflections

What concludes our volume are reflections and practical guidance for those new to convening and facilitating transformative conversations. Such communication strategies are the starting place for change, acknowledging the power of human communication to clarify thought, connect people and ideas, and provide the opportunity for persuasion. Here we reflect on the nature of communicating, the practice of facilitating, and the "how to" of starting campus conversations.

Our hope is that our conversations will convince you to join us in a genuine revitalization movement of a learning enterprise that is now too often disparaged. What we seek are conversations that use the transformative power of *learning* to ensure for ourselves and our students lives well lived.

Why Can't We Talk about the Mess We're In?

JOINING THE CONVERSATION: SUSAN CAMPBELL BALDRIDGE, coauthor of *The College Stress Test* and former provost of Middlebury College

Lori: We really need to talk, though talking somehow sounds much easier than it really is, something I discovered as a child. I remember becoming keenly aware of things that were happening that the grown-ups were not talking about. One of those glaring examples was that my parents were divorced, yet in the hills and woods and churches of southern Indiana in the early seventies, the word *divorce* was never spoken in my hearing. It didn't seem to exist, yet somehow I was living it. And that word was just the beginning of a long list of taboo topics like racism, war, mental illness, and more—all obvious realities of significant import for which I didn't yet have words, and all off-limits in conversation.

Having raised children of my own, I know that well-meaning adults intended to protect me, hoping I would maintain a view of the world that was less complex and less troubled than it really was. No doubt, on topics from Santa Claus to sexuality, many parents struggle with the timing of "the talk." As one of the grown-ups now, I've probed my mother's memory about these matters. She recalls that when I was 12, she asked me if I "had any questions" and I responded, quite definitively, "Not that I want answers to."

As an adolescent, I read Paul Watzlawick's *How Real Is Real?* and began to develop a conceptual understanding about how our communication with one another shapes our reality. Watzlawick begins with this premise:

> Communication creates what we call reality. At first glance this may seem a most peculiar statement, for surely reality is what is, and communication is merely a way of expressing or explaining it. . . . What there are, in fact, are many different versions of reality, some of which are contradictory, but all of which are the results of communication. . . . [The] close connection between reality and communication is a relatively new idea. Although physicists and engineers long ago solved the problems of transmitting signals effectively, and although linguists have for centuries been engaged in exploring the origin and structure of language, and semanticists have been delving into the meanings of signs and symbols, the pragmatics of communication—that is, the ways in which people can drive each other crazy and the very different world views that can arise as a consequence of communication—have become an independent area of research only in the past decades.
> (Watzlawick 1976)

With that reading, I began a lifelong habit of noticing the power of the words we use to speak and to think, as well as the conversations we have or don't have. My fascination with the topic of communication grew as I became an undergraduate student. A struggling "first generation" class-mate shared that *college* was not a word that was spoken to him as a child. That same year, in an Introduction to Psychology class, I integrated the concept of "cognitive dissonance," which helped me better understand why some topics may have been avoided and other questions deemed off-limits. If beliefs and actions clash, how do we explain either, to ourselves—or a curious child? I also came to understand how probing areas of disso-nance is, for intellectuals, not only a fruitful habit but sometimes a sport of sorts. Especially in the liberal arts, these kinds of queries can lead to fascinating work on the general puzzle of being human. And yet, such robust inquiry about the puzzles within our own enterprise of higher edu-cation seem much less common.

It's way past time for those of us in higher education to have "the talk" about these unspeakables. Though we may be discouraged by how others speak and think about us, we are not children needing to be sheltered. Instead, we are leaders and shapers, impacting the economy and well-being of society. We need to ask just why is it that we find ourselves feeling helpless and overwhelmed when others see us as so privileged and powerful. The answer may be because much of the work we do to shape society occurs indirectly, through our students who learn from us how to reason well, how to move from curiosity through the scientific method to discovery, and how to engage ethically as global citizens. Eventually, when we hear about the accomplishments of alumni, our daily work is validated.

Bob: But are we also, perhaps, just a little too willing to believe it is sufficient to rest in our general awareness of the cumulative impact of higher education on human history? Maybe we are taking inordinate comfort in being among the contributors to this expansive enterprise, comfort that fuels inertia.

Lori: Maybe, yet the impact of our work is real. Earlier this week as I was entering my parking garage, I had to brake for a group of prospective students dashing across the street on their way to a visit-day. Their eagerness and energy represent so much of what provides purpose to all of us in higher education. Their mere presence gave me a needed jolt of encouragement and reassurance. In my opening remarks to faculty this year, I earnestly proclaimed that at this moment in our history as a nation, there is no more important role than that of educator. Even as I hear the echo of my own words, I don't want to use that affirmation to construct a reality that is so comfortable that I become complacent, as an individual or an academic leader. I know all too well our collective habit of looking the other way just when we need to do the opposite. It's clear to me that we need to see and speak about all that is real if we are to have any hope of changing things.

In her book *Dare to Lead*, Brené Brown describes these difficult conversations we avoid as "rumbles."

The word *rumble* has become more than just a weird *West Side Story* way to say, "Let's have a real conversation, even if it's tough." It's become a serious intention and a behavioral cue or reminder. A rumble is a conversation defined by a commitment to lean into vulnerability, to stay curious and generous, to stick with the messy middle of problem identification and solving, to take a break and circle back when necessary, to be fearless in owning our parts, and, as psychologist Harriet Lerner teaches, to listen with the same passion with which we want to be heard. (Brown 2018)

It is just this kind of conversation that can bring about change. If you are among the thousands living your professional lives on one of the 4,300-plus campuses in the United States, how often are you avoiding rather than rumbling? What we clearly need is more of the latter, more colleagues wondering what they can actually do to make a difference in the midst of such a mess.

Here are three questions we together need to address—*now*:

1. What are the taboo topics we must broach and with whom, in order to make possible a sustainable revitalization of our enterprise?
2. Which of our communication habits are leading us astray?
3. Where is the cognitive dissonance for us as a collective, and how can we mine it as responsible intellectuals?

Bob: You make painfully clear how most discussions of the mess we are in focus on the pieces of the problem—disheartening scandals, forgotten commitments, and lots of examples of underperformance. Too few of us are prepared to argue that the separate pieces reveal a problematic whole, what might be best described as a loss of sanctuary. Colleges and universities are no longer viewed as special places—no longer revered or celebrated for their unfettered commitment to learning.

Susan Baldridge, then Middlebury's provost, was responsible for drafting the chapter in *The College Stress Test* that focused on how college closings are being talked about. Ultimately, she came to understand that there are three different, and largely disconnected, conversations taking place about higher education and its future. The first belongs to the pundits, who seem to be taking a perverse delight in predicting that upward of half the nation's colleges and universities face near imminent closure. Then there is what Baldridge labeled "the language of elegiac grief," in which those who dwell in institutions that have either closed or are about to close talk about their loss of a future.

> The fact that the language of institutional closure so closely parallels the well-understood stages of grief is all the evidence we need of people's affection for and connection to their particular college or university and of their belief in the exceptional nature of these institutions. In the character of this grief, then, we see the explanation for the disconnect between public conjectures about the dismal future of higher education and the more localized optimism about a particular school's immunity to the general malaise. It is precisely because each school matters so much to its people that conversations about risk are so hard to have. What is needed is a reconciliation between these two discourses, one that precedes the need for elegies and obituaries and, instead, points to the strategies for accurately diagnosing and acknowledging an institution's actual condition. (Zemsky, Shaman, and Baldridge 2020)

Lori: Between the grievers and the pundits reside higher education's leaders, people in roles like mine, generally intent on providing institutional reassurance, proclaiming often and loudly that "everything's gonna be all right." Or as Baldridge observed,

> The conversation taking place on most college and university campuses is noticeably different. In fact, if you diagnosed the well-being of higher education based on the public comments and missives of presidents around the country, you would conclude that the patient is largely in good health. Most such accounts have a fairly positive outlook to offer: College X is thriving. University Y is optimistic about the future. School Z is redirecting efforts with a bold new strategy. These messages intentionally link the school's distinctive history and mission with a promise of exciting opportunities and long-term vibrancy. (Zemsky, Shaman, and Baldridge 2020)

Bob: Susan was also a colleague who joined us on our Noah's Ark project involving nearly one of every kind of institution—or so it seemed at the time. What that effort yielded were not only friendships that will continue to supply intellectual sustenance but a monograph that sought to make sense of the undergraduate curriculum. I have invited Susan to add her voice here, and she has weighed in by first observing that you and I often talk a lot about the academy's collective reticence, as well as the urgent need for collective conversations.

Susan Baldridge: Here I would add that it can be difficult for institutional leaders to know how and where to start. Lori's claim that "there is no more important role than that of educator" is one with which most on a college or university campus would agree. But that statement leaves unquestioned what we each believe is inherent in that role. What are the necessary qualities, characteristics, and behaviors of educators? What are the practices that allow us to best achieve our goals for students? How are these characteristics and practices different now than they might have been in the past? As much agreement as one might find with the broad claim about our value as educators, I venture that there would be much less agreement in response to those more specific questions. In fact, these are topics that academics and those who devote their lives to higher education see as central not only to their institution's identity, but to their own. But this, of course, is precisely why such conversations—difficult as they may be—are necessary, even urgent.

And as you suggest, the "rumble-y" nature of these conversations is precisely why we are so reticent to have them. Who wants to begin a conversation when it's likely to be fraught with anger, frustration, and threats to my worldview? One tactic used by facilitators trying to move a conflicted group to consensus is to "name the resistance in the room." What is being challenged here? What is at stake in this conversation? I would posit that naming the fears and source of resistance is one key to framing these discussions. In the words of Lori's 12-year-old self, these conversations will address questions we may not want to hear the answers to, and we would do well to acknowledge that.

Many have correctly argued that collective change—and the necessary conversation that must precede it—is foreign to the academy. Some of that is due to active resistance for the reasons we've been naming here. But I'll add that there is also a simple lack of experience with this kind of change on most campuses. For many decades, the majority of institutions have remained largely the same. There has been remarkable consistency over time in our basic structures, practices, and principles. Not surprisingly then, as a whole, members of our communities have become accustomed to the status quo, and our leaders have little experience with how to guide an institution through an exercise in transformation. And as people who have made our careers being experts in our chosen fields, acknowledging that we don't know what we're doing or how to proceed is deeply distressing. To refer back to Brené Brown, we must make "a commitment to lean into vulnerability," allowing that we may simply not be sure where these conversations will take us.

Bob: Susan comes naturally to this juncture having contributed to our work originally titled "Is It Closing Time?" When the volume's publisher, Johns Hopkins University Press, objected to that title, the three authors, myself included, acquiesced after it was pointed out to us that no college or university president would want to be seen walking across campus carrying under his or her arm a book whose title was "Is It Closing Time?"

That, in a nutshell, is the problem. Almost everyone with a major leadership role senses that a truly frank conversation, warts and all, will do little more than give succor to the academy's detractors. Instead, we are asked to carry on, burying our mistakes and reassuring ourselves that what we do is as important as it is worthwhile.

Lori: That's not the kind of "sanctuary" we seek, right? You and I are saying loudly and plainly we need instead to *rumble*. Without sustained conversation, there will be neither reform nor revitalization.

Bob: What we need to do now is to define the nature of the conversation American higher education requires if it is to sustain itself in an era of change, disruption, and dislocation. You come closest to asking exactly the right question when you focus on the collective we. Though it is easy to conclude all of higher education is in the same boat, the larger reality is that almost no one really believes we are. Indeed, across the enterprise the problem is a missing sense of "we" as in "we the people" or "we the professoriate" or more simply "we the members of the same college community." The kind of collective change you are advocating is now foreign to the academy. It is something we could do but seem not to have the stamina to pursue, no matter how great the need. "How do we change that?" you might ask, and the answer you have correctly promoted is "by having continuing conversations that engage the whole enterprise."

Lori: Continuing conversations are key, yet at the same time we need to be clear as to the subjects of those conversations. The broader issues impacting higher education may seem tangential to the everyday work in a specific department or discipline, or on our particular campus. Can individuals longing for a different order of things propel systemic transformation? There are guides to structuring the work of systemic change. In 2011, John Kania and Mark Kramer described what they call the "collective impact" approach to bringing about systemic change rather than focusing on isolated impact within a hyperlocalized setting. One of the conditions for success in this framework is "continuous communication," a practice more recently refined and described by collective impact scholars as "authentic and inclusive community engagement" (Walzer and Weaver 2019).

The scholarship of teaching and learning, and the creation of active learning classrooms are two important movements challenging traditions within the academy and reaching across campus contexts. There are also local, high-impact initiatives with broad applicability like the Red House at Georgetown, modeling the inclusion of students to generate transformative practice, as well as various restorative justice and campus sustainability initiatives. These endeavors—along with many others— show us that both influence leaders from within a context and boundary-crossing communication networks are critical elements of transformation, just as Everett M. Rogers argues in his classic work, *Diffusion of Innovations* (Rogers 1962/2003). As an epigraph to the first chapter of the fifth edition, Rogers uses a quotation from Machiavelli's *The Prince*: "There is nothing more difficult to plan, more doubtful of success, nor more dangerous to manage than the creation of a new order of things."

Cathy Davidson in the introduction to her book *The New Education*, reinforces that sentiment with a statement with which few if any will disagree: "It will not be easy to transform the university from the inside" (Davidson 2017). As a member of a faculty team that created a dramatic reform of general education at a regional comprehensive university, I made several academic conference presentations about the endeavor. Invariably, after I described the intricacies of the new program, many hands would go up. While I wished to be asked about the impact of Quest III courses on students' civic engagement or the retention-building peer mentor program, no such luck. Instead of inquiring about *what* we did, nearly everyone asked about the *how*. Some were incredulous. "How in the world could you make that happen?" Others were skeptical, sharing some familiar storyline such as, "That could never work on my campus because the chairs of history and English have been protecting their lib ed requirement turf for decades. We all know nothing is going to change until one of them retires or dies." Aware that the "how" of transformative communication within the academy is rarely revealed, I eventually crafted a new presentation called "The Very Secret Diaries of General Education Reform." While that humorous framing resonated with academics, the general public would likely be surprised to learn about the monumental effort necessary to enact even incremental change in the curriculum or pedagogy.

Bob: And as challenging and important as it may be, gen ed is only one element of a massive system in need of monumental change, only one piece of a 10,000-piece puzzle. It is not uncommon for the enterprise's leadership to voice similar concerns about the process for moving forward collectively. Speculating about the likelihood of things changing for the better in *The Struggle to Reform Our Colleges*, former Harvard president Derek Bok describes a "pervasive lack of knowledge about *how* to proceed" (Bok 2017). Senior scholar emerita at the Carnegie Foundation for the Advancement of Teaching and Learning Mary Taylor Huber observes that even the inspirational Cathy Davidson "says relatively little about . . .

how change on a larger scale might occur" (Huber 2019). Even as Bok points to innovations that are working in isolated pockets, he observes that "the greatest obstacles to progress occur . . . when proven reforms need to spread through the system" (Bok 2017).

Lori: Bok, Huber, Kania, Kramer, Rogers, along with the authors of *Making Sense of the College Curriculum* (Zemsky, Wegner, and Duffield 2018), all point to the same grand challenge. As members of the academy with varying roles, we may be devoting our entire professional careers to the careful construction of a corner section of that 10,000-piece puzzle, never even conversing with those working on another corner. I recently met a wildly successful education innovator who revealed her highest career aspiration—to have at least 20 percent of the classrooms on her campus equipped for active learning. Thinking about how much more widely her reforms need to be diffused, my heart skipped a beat as I experienced a moment of cognitive dissonance that needs our mutual inquiry. As educators leading the collective learning of a whole society from within a sector that holds research in the highest esteem, what is it that keeps us from applying education research to practice broadly? In his powerful book of stories, *What the Best College Teachers Do*, Ken Bain concludes that to progress as a collective,

> we can begin to think of ourselves as a learning university concerned with the learning of both faculty (research) and students (teaching) and the ways in which the learning of one can benefit the other. . . . [We need] a recognition that efforts to foster learning in others can stimulate our own greater understanding. It is a commitment . . . to building and sustaining a community of learners. At its core, such a community is defined by engagement . . . sustaining the community and its conversations. (Bain 2004)

Earlier, you lamented that perhaps we in higher education are no longer revered or celebrated for our unfettered commitment to learning, a change that has led to a loss of what you fondly called "sanctuary."

Bob: Just lamenting that loss won't change anything. Nor will angry shouts at those, both within and without the academy, who delight in our discomfort. The answer instead is that we need to ask, "How do we revitalize that identity, for the good of the whole?"

Lori: At a recent national gathering of higher education leaders, author Tara Westover reminded us that "the ability to hear and integrate many ideas, many histories, and many points of view is at the heart of what it means to be 'educated'" (Westover 2019). Among those of us privileged to be highly educated and to work within the context that provides such education for others as its core mission, truly educational conversations that straddle the research-teaching divide and that connect us across disciplines, roles, and campuses are routinely missing.

Susan Baldridge: Lori's point that even small changes often require monumental efforts is, I'm afraid, all too familiar for many who work in higher education. As I wrote of my own similar experiences in a recent blog post, "I recall a colleague who was opposing a proposed change to the structure of several departments—a change that he felt called into question his past and future contributions. Although the process had involved years (literally years) of meetings and votes, as it neared its conclusion, he said to me, 'Susan, this is all happening with *baffling* speed.' These conversations can be tests of endurance." Consistent with Ken Bain's observations that you share here, ultimately I came to view this kind of institutional change work, glacially slow though it may sometimes be, as similar to teaching. My goal was to help those in the community become students of the institution, providing them with the resources and information that I felt would illuminate their understanding; we would then debate what it all meant, and how or whether we needed to change as a result. The particular challenge we face is that we must now speed up the transformation of the curriculum to produce the timely change that is needed, even if the speed is baffling to some.

The recent (as of this writing) frantic—and sometimes creative and successful—adaptations made by nearly every academic institution in this country to move students off campus and begin delivering education virtually and remotely in response to the COVID-19 pandemic is a lesson we should not miss the opportunity to highlight. Whether this proves to be the beginning of a more permanent shift to education delivered remotely remains to be seen; but it does represent a poignant example of just what institutions can accomplish when they must. We have the capacity to be nimble when we face a compelling and urgent need. And think how much more successful and creative we might have been had we had just a bit more time to make these changes. Thus, we need to create the appropriate sense of urgency around the vexing issues we have been avoiding and to engage those conversations sooner rather than later.

That said, I feel compelled to note that even when these conversations are challenging and the problems we seek to address are vexing, it is possible to approach them with curiosity and to find moments of joy in the work. Some of the highlights of my professional career have been shared with wonderful, hard-working colleagues as we completed a daunting and effective project. Here is where we can leverage what many of us love most about the work of higher education: there is enormous gratification to be had in tackling and solving the seemingly unsolvable problem, and there is camaraderie to be enjoyed in the teamwork necessary to achieve institutional change. Those who work in higher education are better than anyone at working diligently even when gratification is long delayed. In my conversations with administrative colleagues across the country, these rewards seem to be what keeps them going, even as they slog through the many challenges we are describing. With this book as a call to arms, I believe we can have meaningful, and ultimately successful, conversations, no matter how messy they may be.

Bob: One last observation before we tackle the conversations higher education has successfully avoided. If conversation is, as the three of us have argued, the key to not just a different but a fundamentally better future, who do we expect to convene those conversations?

Some thirty years ago the Pew Charitable Trusts took up that challenge, convening what became known as the Pew Higher Education Roundtable. As chair, I presided over a truly remarkable collection of higher education leaders. We met four times a year, and after each session we issued "Policy Perspectives," a thought paper that was intended to encourage others to have the same conversation we had within the Roundtable. It was a wildly successful effort in no small part because it carried the imprimatur of a well-funded foundation then becoming a major player across American higher education. With further support from the Pew Charitable Trusts, we convened separate roundtables on more than 150 college and university campuses. When Pew ended its funding after nine years, the effort was taken up and supported for another three years by the Knight Foundation.

I tell this story now not as an example of an abiding success, though it did spur interesting conversations for more than a dozen years, but rather as an example of how hard it is to sustain such efforts. Today the Roundtable is largely forgotten. The campuses that convened their own roundtables have moved on. While the effort was responsible for some important additions to the higher education landscape, we fell far short of sparking the revitalization movement we had in mind.

Lori: What you did together in the Roundtable provides a hopeful model for the structure of influential conversations, in a time when hopefulness is no longer the norm (even among us optimists). I remember a 24-hour period when I simply could not escape thinking about the mess we were in, even before COVID-19. It began with a quick glance at my Facebook feed before bed. There was a recycled post by a local high school junior declaring that college was no longer necessary. I started to scroll through the hundreds of comments for some glimmer of hope. When none appeared, I turned out the light. At 4:00 a.m. I was awake again checking the *Chronicle* as I do every weekday morning. That day's headline? "It's an Aristocracy—What the Admissions-Bribery Scandal Has Exposed about Class on Campus." No better was its companion: "Public Colleges Seek Ways to Pull Up the Welcome Mat for White-Nationalist and Other Extremist Speakers." Looking for something a bit more uplifting, I checked the paid article; sometimes that section holds inspirational ideas. That day's focus? The campus "addictions crisis." After a caffeine-fueled yoga session to fortify myself for the day, I began my drive to campus across southeastern Minnesota's beautiful bluff country and turned on the radio, preset for news. Topic? The student loan crisis. Predictably, a local barista was venting about his overwhelming debt and useless philosophy degree. I turned off the radio, swerved to avoid a deer, and eventually pulled into my parking space.

Just the day before, I'd received next year's draft budget from the System office revealing that a request for investment to grow enrollment on my still new campus would not be fully funded. This disappointing news came after more than a year of strategic planning, listening sessions, collaborative proposal drafts and re-drafts, wisdom-seeking from colleagues and policymakers, and a well-received and formally endorsed proposal to the Board of Regents. Why did professional colleagues of goodwill and stellar character make such decisions? They saw few other alternatives in light of declining state appropriations. Even with a governor authentically committed to education, the legislative session ended with the university receiving much less than it requested or needed. Those disappointments, of course, translate into real pain for the academic units. And now, with the COVID-19 pandemic, dramatic revenue loss and enrollment ambiguities have moved higher education from a more general mess to a potential catastrophe.

Even in this new state of disruption that is compelling us to adapt rapidly, I'm worried that some of us in the academy think of ourselves as powerless to bring about lasting change and yet—*revitalization is possible*. An example from another context might prove provocative. Early in his best seller, *Being Mortal*, Atul Gawande tells the story of Bill Thomas from upstate New York who, much to his surprise, ended up at Harvard. When he graduated with a freshly minted MD, he returned home and took up a position as medical director at Chase Memorial Nursing Home. What he encountered there were the three plagues of nursing home existence: boredom, loneliness, and helplessness. Blocked by an environment that made safety and regulation more of a priority than their patients' need for lives well-lived, Thomas convinced himself that only something truly different would change a nursing home's culture. With a little help from his wife, Jude, he knew what to seek: a grant from the state of New York that would bring animals, birds, plants, and children into Chase in truly large numbers. When the proposal was funded, the transformation began. Here it helps to let Gawande tell the rest of his story:

This task was not small. Every place has a deep-seated culture as to how things are done. "Culture is the sum total of shared habits and expectations," Thomas told me. As he saw it, habits and expectations had made institutional routines and safety greater priorities than living a good life and had prevented the nursing home from successfully bringing in even one dog to live with the residents. He wanted to bring in enough animals, plants, and children to make them a regular part of every nursing home resident's life. Inevitably the settled routines of the staff would be disrupted, but then wasn't that part of the aim?

"Culture has tremendous inertia," he said. "That's why it's culture. It works because it lasts. Culture strangles innovation in the crib."

To combat the inertia, he decided they should go up against the resistance directly—"hit it hard," Thomas said. He called it the Big Bang. They wouldn't bring a dog or a cat or a bird and wait to see how everyone responded. They'd bring all the animals in more or less at once.

That fall, they moved in a greyhound named Target, a lapdog named Ginger, the four cats, and the birds. They threw out all their artificial plants and put live plants in every room. Staff members brought their kids to hang out after school. . . . It was shock therapy.

An example of the scale: they ordered the hundred parakeets for delivery all on the same day. . . . It was "total pandemonium," Thomas said. The memory of it still puts a grin on his face. . . .

"We didn't know what the heck we were doing. *Did, Not, Know* what we were doing." Which was the beauty of it. They were so patently incompetent that most everyone dropped their guard and simply pitched in—the residents included. . . .

They had to solve numerous problems on the fly. . . .

All sorts of crises occurred, any one of which could have ended the experiment. One night at 3:00 a.m., Thomas got a phone call from a nurse. . . . "The dog pooped on the floor," the nurse said. . . . "Are you coming to clean it up?" As far as the nurse was concerned, this task was far below her station.

She didn't go to nursing school to clean up dog crap. . . . The next morning, when he arrived, he found that the nurse had placed a chair over the poop, so no one would step in it, and left.

Some of the staff felt that professional animal wranglers should be hired. . . . Others believed that, just as in anyone's home, the animals were a responsibility that everyone should share. . . . It was a battle over fundamentally different worldviews: Were they running an institution or providing a home? (Gawande 2017)

Bob: What a wonderful story, joyously told by a master storyteller. More than that, the story is something of a parable for higher education and the plight of those who would change the inertia of the academy's restricting culture. Read the story again. In your mind, substitute the word *student* for *resident* and *faculty* for *staff*. The cats, dogs, birds, plants, and children become an endless chain of pedagogical experiments. The big substitution, of course, is *learning* for *living*. And it takes little imagination to transpose the nurse's comment about dog poop to one by a senior faculty member who declares with disdain, "I didn't go to graduate school to cater to Gen Z and their technology addiction."

Lori: Bob, when I first suggested the title for our book, you were not impressed. You asked if I was aware that it has two meanings. "Yes!" I exclaimed, with enthusiasm. "That's why I love it so much." To move past the current mess to a Big Bang of systemic change, we must initiate a rumble of conversation about topics we tend to avoid and across roles that so often divide us. To do so is the best hope we have for influencing the direction and thus the future of this great enterprise of higher education.

Are you and your colleagues ready? Bob and I challenge you to launch your first campus conversation with the core question of this chapter: *What are the taboo topics our campus community must broach and with whom, in order to make possible a sustainable revitalization of our enterprise?* Let's rumble!

Will a Commitment to Community Actually Move Us Forward?

JOINING THE CONVERSATION: TERI PIPE, chief well-being officer, Arizona State University

Lori: The Zumbro River meanders through the bluffs of southern Minnesota, twisting incessantly on its way north to the Mississippi. As I write on this sunny November morning, I'm looking out my window watching the middle fork of that river freeze gradually before my eyes. On the other side, trees on a high bluff are releasing their yellow leaves. They seem to dance as they descend to the river—some sink, some freeze in place, some find the open water and float downstream. I love this view and relish the momentary, soul-feeding solitude.

A few years ago we held a student event on this river, one that has now become an annual tradition. The original idea was to create a meaningful experience for a group of students that were the first cohort of a pilot program, Health CORE. The students had been selected for this "Community of Respect and Empowerment" based on their academic potential, common purpose, commitment to success, and diversity. New to college and each other, they would be signing a covenant to live, learn, and lead together. On that first day, we asked them to launch their rental kayaks from a small town upstream and paddle their way down to my backyard, using the journey as a metaphor for the transition from high school to college, from individual to community, and from where they had been to wherever they were going in life.

Those students will graduate this coming spring, and each has a story about that day. Some were paralyzed by fear. Some former city dwellers capsized and climbed a bluff expecting wilderness, only to find a helpful anesthesiologist puttering in his garage. Some paddled steadily. One finished in half the time as the others. And owing to a deluge of rain the night before this adventure, all faced the challenge of getting out of the river in deep mud and pulling their kayaks up a steep hill. Some laughing, some crying, they eventually found themselves seated on the floor of my home, ready to reflect. I watched as the skilled faculty facilitator guided their processing, listening intently from my corner perch by the fireplace as insights and bonds began to form in the lively conversation. Eventually she asked them, "How do you expect to navigate the unknown as you move forward in your journey?" That room full of mud-crusted, sunburned, 18-year-old human potential fell quiet. After a long pause, the wise professor said firmly and with conviction, "You've got to find your people."

Student development professionals and experiential learning designers will not be surprised to learn that the students in this trailblazing group, now seniors, are excelling in GPA and timely degree completion in conjunction with other key variables like sense of belonging, well-being, resilience, peer accountability, self-regulation, social engagement, and intercultural competence. This pilot of a full-blown cohort structure for coursework, community engagement, and residential life is set to become the norm for our future students. Through their hundreds of conversations since that first day together, these students have knit together a sustaining community. Though highly diverse in many ways, that inaugural class of Health CORE students now all share a common identity as well, and they are each quick to claim, in one way or another, "I wouldn't have made it to this moment without my people."

Bob, you and I are not 18, not at the beginning of our journeys by a long stretch. And I have already revealed that I find moments of solitude nourishing. And clearly, though such programs may exist, most new faculty and staff don't participate in a bonding expedition with their colleagues as part of their orientation. Do we and others like us in higher education really need to "find our people" to be well, both individually and collectively?

Bob: Lori, it is another great story but I fear it takes us in the wrong direction. The community I want to spur is the campus community writ large— of which students are a part, but more as transient participants than sustaining members. Still, I think your story illustrates two important aspects of the problem. First, responsibility for organizing student communities lies outside the community itself. In your story, it is a faculty facilitator in partnership with a group of student development professionals who take the lead and ultimately are given credit for the exercise's success. In the campus communities I want us to focus on, external direction is rarely available and seldom sought. Second, the central focus in your story is a physical event—successfully navigating the river, which in your story is treated as something of a parable illustrating the power of community purpose. There was, as you report, a vivid sharing of stories among the participants but not necessarily a sustaining conversation. In contrast we have declared ourselves interested primarily in sustaining conversations that involve a substantial commitment to truth telling.

Hence my questions: Why across so many academic communities are there so few sustaining conversations about mission and collective purpose? Why does the academy make student communities both a program and a budget priority while investing so little in fostering shared faculty and staff endeavors? When, for example, was the last time that navigating a river, either actually or metaphorically, became a shared faculty experience? And when was the last time that there was a broadly organized campus conversation focusing on how and why higher education needs to change and the campus's role in promoting that commitment to change?

In part the answer lies in the changing nature of academic communities. When I came to Penn in the 1960s with a newly minted PhD from Yale, I joined a community of like-minded academics that was homogenous, male-centered, and ordinarily heterosexual. The goal was to live as close to campus as possible, where the schools were nearby and the housing was often more interesting. We didn't so much talk; rather, we entertained, the dinner party serving as our principal excuse to gather. I had a colleague who regularly reminded me that we were living lives seemingly right out of Edward Albee's *Who's Afraid of Virginia Woolf?* More prosaically, he would also point out that what made our close-knit circle of colleagues possible were stay-at-home wives and partners who tended the children as well as their husbands.

All that has changed. Gender balance has yielded a host of dual-income families who often choose to live near her work rather than his. Indeed the professoriate is now closer to mirroring student demographics, though faculty-of-color are still underrepresented. The shifts in the market for an undergraduate education in which the rich have gotten richer and the big bigger, has yielded an exaggerated gap in the economic well-being of some but certainly not all faculty. Those at now under-resourced institutions are irritated by what they perceive as an economically driven devaluation of their efforts and institutions. There is some evidence that those at top-rated institutions are nervous as well, though for understandably different reasons, more often tied to the new nature of the competition for tenured positions and research funding—all in all a set of conditions for making college communities the antithesis of happy places.

Lori: Bob, your reference to the close-knit community you enjoyed in the early days of your faculty career got me thinking about my launch into the academy. Your recollections are probably doing the same for readers who are contrasting their experience with yours, based on the historical context in which they began, their roles in the academy, their specific campus and region of the country, their cultural and socioeconomic backgrounds, and more.

As a new faculty member in 1991, I received a beautiful, printed invitation to attend something called "Faculty Dames." Having moved across the country to take the position (the only advertised opportunity focused on my specialty in communication education), my social calendar was rather open that first semester. Curious about the unusual name, I arrived at the address—an older home sitting oddly, right in the middle of the campus. Inside, tea service was set on lace doilies and gloved, gray-haired women were pouring. They welcomed me warmly, explaining that they had organized Faculty Dames decades ago to connect the wives of faculty. They were dear friends, and as their husbands were retiring (and passing away), these connections and conversations over tea continued to be a meaningful part of their lives. In this homogenous community, they had found "their people." But as their numbers shrank, these women agreed to invite new female faculty to join their group. I was the only one who showed up. Though the Faculty Dames community did not continue, their spirit of hospitality lingered in the house when two decades later it transitioned into the teaching and learning center in which faculty conversations flourished, community was crafted, and sustained change was ignited. Bob, that was the house where I first met you. There you facilitated a powerful conversation with a group of diverse campus change agents.

It's fascinating to look back on our careers in higher ed, to reflect on how community formed or why, more typically, it did not form. People enter in such different ways, from postdoc to a tenure-track role, from undergraduate student to residential hall director charged with teaching a first-year seminar, from adjuncting at four campuses to an annually renewable appointment in a grant-dependent lab, from corporate to a campus context. The list goes on and on. Consequently, there are vast differences. Those using our interaction as a catalyst for their conversation can add stories about how they attempt to connect with others in their specific campus environments; how they create and cope with campus cultures that are more or less inclusive and welcoming; how forming communities with people at other institutions has contributed to their well-being; and how they ultimately experience a connection (or lack of connection) to the broader enterprise of higher education.

To be sure, community doesn't just happen. If it did, we wouldn't have the "loneliness" epidemic that Pew Research Center and others have documented. Health CORE students didn't become a community because they paddled a river together once, nor are faculty in a specific department automatically a community because they share space and a discipline (as anyone in a dysfunctional department can attest!). Instead, communities are crafted over time, knit together, really, through sustained conversations that ultimately expand the identities of those who participate. Though community may be rarer than we wish in higher ed, I have had the joy of experiencing the power of transformative communities several times in my life. Two come to mind just now, flooding me with cherished memories—of a specific group of people to whom I belonged for a time—and the constructive changes that emanated from our interaction. First, there was a "dream team" of diverse colleagues who conversed over many weekends (and various types of beverages, depending on the time of day) in a collective quest to revitalize general education. And the other was a somewhat random collection of my intercultural communication students who bonded and challenged one another as we lived for a brief time with a remote tribe in the Amazon rainforest, navigating cultural ambiguity together. In both of these memorable communities, it was clear to me that it was *conversation* that creates that coveted sense of belonging, essential to individual and collective well-being.

Bob: I confess to being surprised that when moved to comment specifically on the diminished sense of community across the academy, we both chose to focus on changes in the social contexts that are changing communities everywhere. And perhaps that national drift, what you referenced as a loneliness epidemic, alone accounts for the transformation of faculty lives and expectations. My guess, however, is that the answer we are looking for is more complex, more explicitly tied to what universities do—and in fact do very well.

In offering an expanded explanation I would start with what has happened to the knowledge base for which universities are principally responsible. In terms of our research nearly everyone is now a specialist who knows more and more about less and less. Our academic lives are being sliced into evermore separate and discrete pieces out of which too few of us ever try to fashion a compelling whole. My favorite indicator of our changed world of work is the difficulty that appointment and promotion committees have in judging the academic quality of a candidate's portfolio. The lament often heard is that "none of us knows enough about the candidate's specialty to render a considered judgment." That was simply not the case forty or more years ago. The message, whether intended or not, is that each of us is now on our own.

At the same time, collaborations among faculty are as likely to be across as within institutions. You are at the University of Minnesota Rochester; I am still at Penn. The research team responsible for *Making Sense of the College Curriculum*, in addition to you and me, included Greg Wegner of the Great Lakes College Association and Ann Duffield, now an independent contractor but formerly the head of university relations at Penn. Almost all big projects and most small and midsize ones are similarly composed of colleagues drawn from a host of physically separated campuses. Hard to build a sustaining community when so many of your team's members are scattered about, though with the current global pandemic many of us are really working at it. To be sure, it's even more difficult to launch sustaining conversations that involve more than the immediate work team itself.

My point is pretty simple—the tides are against us. If we want to have sustaining conversations involving colleagues from across an institution we will need to work doubly hard to overcome the forces of disaggregation. The larger irony is that in spite of these obstacles we continue to rhetorically celebrate the importance of community. It is a message that makes for elegant campaign statements but not much else. We really need to do better.

Lori: I don't think we have much disagreement about the need to do better. Instead, the question is, *how* can we do better? How do we build a community that enhances the well-being of individuals and the whole enterprise of higher education? If we are to flourish, individually and collectively, and if we are to simultaneously deliver on our promise that education elevates the human experience for all, new communication habits are necessary. And yes, in a culture that has long celebrated individualism, collective thought and action are likely to be resisted.

I remember first hearing the term *glocal* in a stimulating conversation about environmental issues. Faculty in that extended dialogue were shaping both a new environmental studies curriculum and a new facility, aspiring to be a model. Their aims required them to expand the notion of "we" to include building contractors, policymakers, students, financial decision makers, and others. The compelling notion of the faculty in those sustained conversations was that ideas needed to have both local and global implications (as well as implementation processes). While that mantra to *think globally and act locally* is no longer new, it has yet to be applied to a broad process for changing higher education.

When it comes to sustained conversations that can build a shared "we," faculty aren't usually seen as the potential leaders of such a movement. It's true that professors often approach their work as independent contractors and in so doing may construct a system antithetical to forming community. Part of what makes me so confident that faculty could lead transformation through community is a long-standing, accepted practice in the academy that could be leveraged as a strength—even in collective bargaining environments. The commitment to service is built into the faculty role and almost always includes assignment to committees to advance the shared aims of departments, colleges, campuses, and disciplines. Nearly all academic CVs expect a structure that itemizes those types of group service. Even the review process for journal article publication is built on group consensus, with multiple reviewers' comments informing the decision to accept or reject. The widely accepted assumption of committee service and the process of group deliberation that takes place in those routine forums—on everything from hiring to curriculum to conference planning to research publication—is that the end result will be better than if an individual, no matter how expert, made the decision-at-hand independently. Of course, even in identifying this strength, let's acknowledge that such committee deliberations are notoriously slow, rarely adopting the "agile" or "sprint" methods now common in other contexts. But that trust in the collective judgment of a group of "us" is a starting place for a systemic change endeavor—you know, one that is glocal. Building on local efforts characterized by trust of the other to engage in civil discourse for enhanced decision making, imagine leveraging social media to scale a collective conversation that propels systemic change. If we trust, if we assume positive intent, if we broaden our inclusion, if we can leverage digital modalities so that scaling up is possible, then a transformative community could emerge. My "ifs" are significant, but with deep respect for all the work that has come before, I just don't see change-at-scale occurring without intentional disruption that forms a shared identity for higher education professionals across campuses and contexts.

Bob, earlier you mentioned the irony that even when communitas is elusive, campus leaders tend to use the word *community* as a rhetorical device meant to conjure up positive feelings. So, what is community, anyway? Inherent in our struggle to create community in higher education is the ambiguity of the overused word itself. Many social scientists continue to explore this nebulous concept that is so central to human flourishing. Among them are David M. Chavis and Kien Lee, writing in Stanford's *Social Innovation Review*:

> "Community" is so easy to say. The word itself connects us with each other. It describes an experience so common that we never really take time to explain it. It seems so simple, so natural, and so human. In the social sector, we often add it to the names of social innovations as a symbol of good intentions (for example, community mental health . . .). But the meaning of community is complex. And, unfortunately, insufficient understanding of what a community is and its role in the lives of people in diverse societies has led to the downfall of many well-intended "community" efforts. Adding precision to our understanding of community can help. . . . It's about people.
>
> First and foremost, community is not a place, a building, or an organization; nor is it an exchange of information over the Internet. Community is both a feeling and a set of relationships among people. People form and maintain communities to meet common needs. Members of a community have a sense of trust, belonging, safety, and caring for each other. They have an individual and collective sense that they can, as part of that community, influence their environments and each other. That treasured feeling of community comes from shared experiences and a sense of—not necessarily the

actual experience of—shared history. . . . This feeling is fundamental to human existence. (Chavis and Lee 2015)

In addition to clarifying that it's the *people* that create community, Chavis and Lee identify several other fundamentals of this multifaceted phenomenon: *People live in multiple communities. Communities are nested within each other. Communities are organized in formal and informal ways.* And then they conclude: "The meaning of community requires more thoughtfulness and deliberation than we typically give it. Going forward, researchers, practitioners, and policymakers must embrace this complexity—including the crucial impact communities have on health and well-being—as they strive to understand and create social change" (Chavis and Lee, 2015).

Bob: Were it so! I stand in awe of your optimism and faith in an idea that I have truly found wanting. I am too often left cold by declarations of fealty to the notion that a commitment to community can, in itself, spark change. For communitas to be the norm for all in the academy, what must come first are a host of tough-minded conversations putting forth practical diagnoses such that the interventions that follow a have a real chance of succeeding.

Lori: I know my midwestern, rural upbringing sets me up to be a bit more trusting and hopeful than might be prudent, but for me, the Health CORE journey is most definitely a parable not just for students, but for us as well. As we navigate toward the unknown future of higher education, we need to rediscover our people, *expanding our identities* to include membership in a great collective of educators with whom we share purpose and *moving to action* by asking ourselves, "Short of a river expedition, how might we become more intentional in building communities that both sustain us and serve as a mechanism for inciting change?"

At this point, Teri Pipe joins our conversation. She is a PhD and RN, serving as Arizona State University's chief well-being officer. Professor Pipe is also founding director of ASU's Center for Mindfulness, Compassion and Resilience. Throughout the pandemic, she and her colleagues have been offering a daily conversation about resilience and mindfulness in higher education, via YouTube.

Teri Pipe: The communities described in this chapter (students navigating a river trip, close-knit mostly male faculty enjoying dinner parties, and the "Faculty Dames") are reminiscent of the past and are characterized by academic role distinctions, insider-outsider designations, and implied hierarchical social structures. From the descriptions, the participants in these social structures enjoyed a sense of belonging and connection that are important elements of community. However, there is also a sense of yearning threaded throughout the chapter; there is a sense that something essential and perhaps grander in scope or depth remains missing. The call to action, "how might we become more intentional in building communities that both sustain us and serve as a mechanism for inciting change?" has recently become even more complex and compelling.

COVID-19 and urgent calls for social justice have pushed the limits of higher education to find new ways to educate, support, and sustain students, faculty, and staff. The COVID-19 pandemic has demonstrated that we must expand the scope of our concern dramatically, to include not only our individual organizations or country, but rather the global community. In some ways, having the pandemic as a common "enemy" has served to unite individuals, groups, and communities. Within the United States, the pandemic has also surfaced the realities of how politically polarized and fractured some of our systems (healthcare, supply chain, governance, etc.) have become. Nested in the context of calls for social change and health justice, the implications for higher education are still emerging and will likely continue to require thoughtful reflection and action. In my view, this is a pivotal moment for higher education to redefine community in more expansive, inclusive, and futuristic ways. It is an opportunity we must not squander.

The current social context coupled with the pandemic are teaching us how elaborately we are connected with humans and animals all around the planet, even at a subcellular level. There is no escaping the patterns of connection, contagion, and spread of the virus from location to location, person to person, community to community. The virus provides a living symbol of how intricate and vast the web of human connection is. Could higher education view learners and learning communities as similarly, yet positively, connected and "contagious?"

- Can we reimagine the structures and processes of the learning environment to include not only physical spaces but also virtual and augmented reality spaces where knowledge and wisdom can be made, shared, and redesigned?
- Instead of viewing subgroups as students, faculty, and staff could we all be simply learners, tied together by a lifelong endeavor to gain, share, and design new knowledge and wisdom?
- Could we intentionally blur distinctions between the university and the town/city/community in which it is located, thereby expanding the definition of who belongs?
- Can we intentionally examine stated and unstated hierarchies, boundaries, and power gradients to explore how these invisible structures may affect participants' sense of belonging and community?
- Can we use knowledge and wisdom to connect rather than divide people?

The post-COVID world will continue to exert pressure on higher education to redesign and reinvent in many ways. One of the most exciting is the opportunity to intentionally reimagine, redefine, and embody community.

Lori: Teri's questions could be the starting place for your next campus conversation. You might also begin with story sharing, as Bob and I did. *When and how did you experience community—or challenges to community— within your higher education context?* We also think the big picture question is worthwhile, given our aim to use these conversations as catalysts for glocal change: "*How might we (on this campus and across higher education) become more intentional in building communities that both sustain us and serve as a mechanism for inciting change?*" Ultimately (and pleasantly), a conversation about community may begin to create a new community among your campus conversation partners.

Bob: And remember, if you're new to hosting and structuring conversation on your campus, check the "Reflections" chapter for more ideas about facilitation and other practicalities.

The Slogans That Ensnare Us

JOINING THE CONVERSATION: JOAN T. A. GABEL, president, University of Minnesota

Bob: As I thought again about our call for open and frank conversations, I came to realize that many across higher education will want to shout back at us, "We don't need to talk more—we are already drowning in slogans and circular arguments." And they will be right. The problem, however, is not argumentative excessiveness, but rather the academy's fondness for weaponized slogans that *end* rather than promote discussion.

Let me begin with an example. There is not a college or university in America that is not rhetorically preoccupied with defining its mission in as many words as possible. Presidents and provosts, along with their faculty colleagues, are all too ready to proclaim that "what we need is a well-defined mission statement." In practice, however, most such statements are lists of either what the institution would like to accomplish in the near future or goals it believes it has achieved in the past. Read lots of mission statements and you quickly discover that (a) they are mostly the same and (b) they vary by decade and fad. I recently sat through a recital of such a statement by a president who took pride in the fact that the institution's mission statement did not offer an endless list of good things to do. Rather, this president declared just three attributes central to the institution's mission: inclusion, diversity, and innovation.

Make no mistake—worthy attributes all, but each reflecting the institution's commitment to remaining au courant. The terms were offered as slogans and not much more. A less passive audience might have wanted a discussion of how the campus had forged its consensus supporting "inclusion, diversity, and innovation" as the university's principal goals and whether there was an operational plan for their achievement. I actually know this university reasonably well. Outside of the faculty involved in the leadership of the institution, most simply are unaware of the statement of university mission—not that they are opposed, though some might have wanted scholarship more prominently recognized, but that they are uninvolved and, truth be known, largely uninterested.

At the same time the three terms—inclusion, diversity, and innovation—have become weaponized across campuses principally by advocacy groups that understand the power of slogans. Public events across the institution are being reshaped to promote equity and inclusion in particular. Presidential searches are being redefined. What troubles me is the amorphousness of what is being promoted and the absence of robust conversations about how best to achieve a campus that promotes equity and inclusion beyond making verbal fealty to those concepts a new litmus test.

Diversity and innovation suffer the same problems—no one is opposed, but only a few know what is meant. Diversity as a goal is being reduced to a handful of demographic measures that sum up an institution's progress in achieving a more equitable distribution of opportunity. What is missing are sustained conversations concerning what diversity means. I am a fan of the work of Beverly Tatum, former president of Spelman College, who knows that in a truly diverse community everyone needs to feel they belong. I keep waiting for the conversation about diversity on a campus working to change its demographic profile to take Tatum seriously. It would help as well if the conversation about diversity and the required sense of belonging was not narrowly defined to promote demographic inclusion.

Finally, innovation is a less politically charged goal and in that way less susceptible to weaponization, but it too lacks meaning and operational commitment. What everyone knows is that innovation is an achievement that is easy to celebrate and almost impossible to promote other than by offering financial support to launch new ideas and projects. Still, no administration wants to be known for being indifferent to innovation.

Hence my list of readily promotable slogans starts with *inclusion, diversity,* and *innovation,* with *mission* serving as an umbrella term. To repeat, what these terms promote is worthwhile—what is not worthwhile is the ease with which advocacy groups have weaponized them to choke off discussion.

Lori: Ouch! You picked three of my favorite words—words that appear in the strategic planning documents of the campus I serve. Our "Grounding Values," crafted over nearly two years of robust discussion with broad campus participation, are listed and defined as follows:

Respect. We value habits of interaction that demonstrate the worth and dignity of each person.

Human potential. We value every person's capacity to learn, develop, imagine, create, and contribute.

Community. We value collective work and a culture of trust that promotes collaboration, problem solving, and partnerships while creating belonging, accountability, and courageous action.

Evidence-based decision making. We value strategic collection and careful assessment of data to inform our choices in all matters, including student learning and development.

And finally—

Diversity and inclusiveness. We value the range of human differences and the active pursuit of varied perspectives.

And then there is our "Vision" statement: "The University of Minnesota Rochester will inspire transformation in higher education through innovations that empower our graduates to solve the grand health challenges of the 21st century." My expectation is that my colleagues and I live these grounding values and design our work plans to focus us in the direction of the vision statement. Position request forms, annual reviews, search processes, campus events, tactical action items, resource allocation decisions, learning outcomes, assessment plans, and more, bring this language to life.

I find myself asking whether these words serve as mere slogans on our campus, choking and constraining us, or if they propel our progress as we grapple together to measure and enhance Tatum's description of belonging for all. And, I did hear you say (more than once) that there is nothing wrong with the words themselves but rather that we can be ensnared by the words if they are *declared without discussion* or if they are *detached from the campus community's way of being.* Points taken.

I'm hopeful (not a surprise) that these words elevate and focus what we do as a campus community, and I know that in committee work my colleagues often pause to wrangle with the application of the grounding values to emerging situations, policies, and procedures. Just this week the traditionally accepted categories of "underrepresented students" (Pell-eligible, first generation, and students of color) were challenged using an equity lens that is more specific to our campus and the healthcare industry that employs our graduates. I like that—and perceived not a *trapping* function but rather another essential learning opportunity. Perhaps that's a key question—Are we equipped to have those ongoing discussions about the words, or do we simply slap them on the website? Stated more succinctly, "Are the words meaningful or meaningless?" What worries me most is the indifference you describe as common.

When I imagine our conversation partners reading your opening serve, I wonder if other administrators are feeling defensive like me while more than a few faculty readers are enjoying a collective head nod, saying, "Yep. That's right! Slogans are simple, and the work is complex." Perhaps some will pause to deconstruct the terms in their strategic plans or to shine a light on the hypocrisy of a campus whose values don't align with the reality of lived experience. Such reactions to administrator-generated mantras could stall progress, for sure—so "sloganing" without broad campus dialogue seems to be a real enemy to progress. And then we're back to the core issue—do we even know how to have deep discussion? And, might it be that reactiveness to or dismissal of mission-slogans is simply one more way to avoid the conversations we don't know how to have? I'm beginning to wonder if facilitation of sustained conversation might be the most important task of campus leaders.

When I think about slogans that ensnare the academy and keep us from interacting in ways that move us forward, two terms come to mind immediately: *academic freedom* and *workforce*. I've heard the words *academic freedom* shut down curricular reform discussions many times in my career. Inertia can sometimes be sustained because almost no one wants to propose something that could be perceived as devaluing that nearly sacred component of the academy. Meanwhile, externally, that same phrase is used by some to fortify the claim that we academics are snooty elites or even unified conspirators driving a specific political agenda. Hop on a blog about faculty tenure and read the comments. Breathe them in and consider what kind of rumble you could facilitate if the commenters were students in your classroom or colleagues preparing to vote on a reform effort.

I've also watched faculty groups bristle and eye roll at any suggestion that they are preparing students for the workforce. If the word *training* is added to the sentence—"training the future workforce"—the speaker's credibility is generally diminished, for surely (the supposition goes) a person who utters such a phrase does not appreciate the value of a liberal arts education to produce engaged citizens who will sustain democracy. A slippery slope in which higher education panders to greedy corporations may even be assumed. Meanwhile, chambers of commerce, economic development agencies, businesses in multiple sectors, philanthropic foundations, nonprofit organizations, and others, use the term *workforce development* routinely in their mission statements, citing well-documented, worrisome trends and projections.

Perhaps these words are less slogans or weapons than they are "triggers" for assumptions that interfere with discourse we need to have. As we asked earlier, if the academy is full of smart people, why do we trip on polarizing words as everyone else does? Might we instead create a rich language of authority and accountability as well as inclusion and equity that serves as a unifying catalyst for transformation? And, could we use such a language to model robust and civil dialogue that includes and acknowledges a much wider set of perspectives?

Bob: Well said. Most slogans across higher education probably started out as triggers that, once taken into battle, became weapons. I want to push our conversation by outlining two responses to your comments. The first is a question of verification. How do you know on your campus that your "grounding values" have real and sustaining impact? The proof cannot be just that they become part of the conversation. The ultimate test has to be demonstrably changed behavior—what your campus does becomes different.

My second response adds two terms to our list of weaponized slogans: *shared governance* and *consensus*. The former has become a catch-all response to administrative initiatives that some faculty don't like, as in "You can't do that because it violates the principle of shared governance." In that context the concept of "shared governance" confers the power of the veto on a subset of the faculty. An outsize commitment to consensus often achieves the same end. Several years ago I watched the faculty at a prestigious college wrestle with procedures governing their once-a-month all faculty meetings. It was an often raucous event in which *Robert's Rules of Order* governed. The problem was that over time a dedicated minority had learned that they could thwart any business by simply offering a "substitute motion." It didn't matter that the business before the house was a carefully crafted report and solution offered by a duly constituted faculty committee. Once the minority offered its substitute motion, it took precedence—what the faculty talked about was not the committee's report but the minority's motion. If eventually the faculty disposed of the substitute motion, it mattered little, since the momentum necessary to consider and pass the committee's original recommendation had been lost, set aside for another day. Any attempt to move away from the strictures imposed by *Robert's Rules* was met with loud cries that what was at stake was the sanctity of shared governance.

My point is that even good ideas like shared governance, once weaponized as in my example, become obstacles to productive conversations and progress.

Lori: Sadly, your faculty governance story is not an outlier. Our conversation partners would likely find it easy to expand the list of such weaponized slogans and tell accompanying (and disheartening) stories of how words ensnare and thus impede progress in their higher ed contexts. I'm convinced that the phrases we've already identified (and those that readers can pile on) are revealing something significant. What we've been seeking are catalysts for sustained conversations that can incite change. What I think we've done here is not only to identify some specific words that ensnare, but more important, to become aware of communication habits that serve as conversation *inhibitors* rather than catalysts. Could it be that even as we proclaim the need for change, we simultaneously, perhaps unconsciously, communicate in ways that subvert progress? Let's look a little more closely not at the slogans or weaponized words but rather at how and why we respond in ways that ensnare us.

Much has been said about trigger-words in contexts that focus on everything from PTSD to politics (for some of us, the notion of trigger-warnings in the classroom has itself become an "academic freedom" trigger). When such words are spoken, triggered individuals react emotionally and then rationalize that reaction. Google the word *triggers*, and you'll see that the most common piece of advice is for people to become conscious—aware—that they are being triggered. Perhaps a good place to start is to make our own lists of words that work that way for us—and then think about the kinds of reactions and rationalizations we employ. (Perhaps that's what we were doing earlier in this conversation.)

A next step to getting out of a trigger-react-rationalize rut is to move from the individual level to the collective. What habitual communication patterns follow the reactions and rationalizations, and how do those behaviors impede systemic transformation? Think again about the Middlebury case, or other experiences in faculty groups, curriculum committees, or strategic planning sessions. What do we do, once triggered? Assign negative intent or blame—and then behave antagonistically to the idea or colleague? Build crisis language and fear, galvanizing resistance? Devolve our thinking to a singular explanation, counter to the cognitive complexity necessary to generate creative solutions? Drop out of the discussion altogether, as though it's not happening—avoiding, even when we could be thought or action leaders?

Early in my faculty career, I had a colleague who, when triggered in department meetings by words or ideas she perceived to devalue her discipline, simply stood up, walked out, and literally slammed the door to further conversation. We became ensnared as she taught us what we could and could not talk about in her presence. While that reaction to a trigger may be unusual, other habitual communication behaviors that metaphorically slam the door on sustained conversation about change are frustratingly quite common.

A few years ago I attended a vibrant, two-week workshop at Harvard with people employed in a wide variety of higher education leadership roles. As you can imagine, it was a wonderful gathering of diverse professionals with a keen appetite to learn and grow. In session after session, day after day, the facilitators used a case study approach, and we engaged in enriching discussions until—near the end of our time together—we began a session titled "The Real Reason People Won't Change." The challenge some of us faced that day was that the conversation was not confined to the case; that is, we didn't stay focused on *other* people who wouldn't change. Instead, we were asked to heighten our awareness of how *we* were resisting change. The requisite vulnerability was extremely uncomfortable for many—or to be more succinct, it got personal. Said one participant, "If I'd known this was going to be a navel-gazing therapy session, I'd have skipped it and gone for a walk." That comment illustrated the change-resistance of a person who self-identified as a campus change agent, an all-too-common contradiction that needs our attention.

Organizational psychologists Robert Kegan and Lisa Lahey, authors of the *Harvard Business Review* article that was the basis for that session, offer an explanation for why people (and organizations) don't change even while they believe themselves to be committed to change:

Resistance to change does not reflect opposition, nor is it merely a result of inertia. Instead, even as they hold a sincere commitment to change, many people are unwittingly applying productive energy toward a hidden *competing commitment*. The resulting dynamic equilibrium stalls the effort in what looks like resistance but is in fact a kind of personal immunity to change. . . .

[This recommended process] challenges the very psychological foundations upon which people function. It asks people to call into question beliefs they've long held close, perhaps since childhood. And it requires people to admit to painful, even embarrassing, feelings that they would not ordinarily disclose to others or even to themselves. Indeed, some people will opt not to disrupt their immunity to change, choosing instead to continue their fruitless struggle against their competing commitments. . . .

People [and campus communities] with the most sincere intentions often unwittingly create for themselves Sisyphean tasks. And they are almost always tremendously relieved when they discover just *why* they feel as if they are rolling a boulder up a hill only to have it roll back down again. Even though uncovering a competing commitment can open up a host of new concerns, the discovery offers hope for finally accomplishing the primary, stated commitment. (Kegan and Lahey 2001)

As these psychologists led us through the session, they returned again and again to the basic premise that overcoming immunity to change starts with uncovering competing commitments and big assumptions—and then taking action to challenge both.

As I work on this puzzle with you, I continue to wonder—if we higher education professionals are committed to change, why do we ensnare ourselves by reacting to slogans and communicating in ways that undermine success? In their work on impediments to change, Kegan and Lahey begin with two questions, the answers to which may be useful for us to attempt to struggle through as we pursue ways to be engaged rather than ensnared.

What is our stated commitment?
 • Systemic transformation is needed in higher education and can be

led from within through sustained conversations about complex issues we often avoid.

What keeps us from realizing that stated commitment?

- We use meaningless buzzwords or defense-raising trigger language to describe complex challenges, inhibiting rather than catalyzing sustained conversation.
- We shut down needed conversations with avoidant or aggressive communicative behaviors that emanate from feeling threatened or devalued.

Bob, now I'll toss it back to you (or perhaps our conversation partners) to suggest some answers to the more difficult questions about the assumptions and countercommitments that may be at the root of how we let slogans ensnare us. We'll revisit those critical questions in the "Reflections" chapter with which we conclude this volume.

Bob: Again you have landed where I least expected to find us. I really thought it was the weaponized slogans that ensnared us. You have now suggested it is not the words being used per se, but a more ingrained habit of misconception that stands in our way. Now I suspect our differences are more likely to focus on how we confront and then disarm those misconceptions. You turn to group and related processes for answers. Hard to argue with that perspective, but I somehow still believe what is missing is a moment of startling clarity—a genuine "aha moment" that undergirds all revitalization movements.

But for now I think we need to be satisfied with having come this far together. What we have is the realization, as in the world of Walt Kelly's cartoon character Pogo, that "we have met the enemy and it is us."

We asked Joan Gabel, president of the University of Minnesota system to draw on her experience as an academic administrator to address the fraught nature of campus discourse.

Joan Gabel: Thank you for inviting me to share insights as part of your "open and frank conversation." As I write this, we are in the midst of the COVID-19 pandemic and George Floyd's tragic death. Such intense times reveal that now, more than ever, we must listen—while also taking thoughtful action to help move us forward together.

"Inclusion, diversity, and innovation," are key words, as is the vocabulary and action that normalizes antiracism. These terms are often represented across higher education's mission statements, but it is up to us to ensure that they are not just slogans. They must represent who we are and must define our next steps and accountability as an institution.

Accordingly, these specific terms encompass two of the five "commitments" in our new Systemwide Strategic Plan—Discovery, Innovation & Impact and Community and Belonging. In sum, the plan's five commitments are positioned squarely at the intersection of our values and action as a university. They represent the spine to which all else is connected, helping us to articulate our vision, as well as provide direction to frame our organizational identity. And with this architecture, we are committed to do more and do better, including to sustain impact, which will evolve over time.

During our systemwide strategic planning process over the past year, I've also enjoyed the opportunity to add a "MN" in front of "intersections," as it is traditional across the state to do with similar words. The commitment "MNtersections" could be viewed as a slogan, but at the core of our plan, it represents the inspiration of our state in helping to improve people and places at world-class levels.

In addition, as a cornerstone of our plan's work, we've embraced the idea of shared governance to support our planning process. I recognize this term has been volleyed back and forth in this particular conversation, but for me, shared governance has been an integral part of finding our unified voice and in achieving such a positive outcome. Moreover, it's been instrumental in working through the challenges posed to the university as a result of the COVID-19 pandemic and in driving safety and security solutions in the aftermath of the George Floyd tragedy.

Lastly, in this new normal, we've found that our important shared engagement also echoes the power of deep conversation. In recent days and months, particularly as a result of social distancing, it seems our collective conversations are deeper and more meaningful. We seem to take fewer things for granted. And, now, more than ever, facilitating these deep conversations among representative viewpoints is one of the most important roles of university leaders and the institutions they serve. And I'm proud of our work as a community to do so.

Bob: Thinking and talking about how campus conversations have been changed by the COVID-19 pandemic may be illuminating. A good place to start new campus conversations may be to list words that usually serve as triggers or traps for you and others, and then to explore any changes you've observed during this time of crisis. Perhaps our shared concern for the greater good will generate fresh opportunities for revitalizing conversation.

· conversation 4

Why Can't We Connect with Each Other?

JOINING THE CONVERSATION: RANDALL BASS, vice president for strategic education initiatives, Georgetown University

Lori: When I was teaching intercultural communication to midwestern undergraduates in the early nineties, I began class with basic questions to determine our starting point. One question became routine: "What are the three major world religions?" Students wrote their answers on cards, which I collected and tallied. Semester after semester, the top three responses to that inquiry were (1) Catholic, (2) Lutheran, and some version of (3) "I don't know." Colleagues from that period of my career can probably still recall me venting about this situation. Many of the students on our regional campus had limited experience connecting across differences, to be sure, but what bothered me most were the students who seemed to lack motivation to expand their awareness when given the opportunity. I changed my pedagogical approach from the Socratic method to simulations—and still encountered slow progress toward the learning outcomes I'd envisioned. "Too bad I can't just drop them all in the jungle, where they'd have to connect across difference to survive," I muttered to an empty classroom after an especially challenging session. Over the years, that sarcastic thought lingered—festered, really—until an idea emerged. When I approached the learning abroad office, a creative staff member helped me discover an early version of what is now a blossoming eco-cultural tourism industry. Ultimately, I found myself near the Amazon with nineteen students, settling into a thatched hut already inhabited by giant moths and spiders. By necessity and our new close proximity to culturally different others, we were motivated to forge connections without a common language. We did that as we ate, worked, and played with members of the tribe. Soccer saved us—because we shared some understanding of the basic rules of the game. The student journals from this trip revealed that both ambiguity and anxiety were primary catalysts for accelerated learning.

By now you know that much of what I've learned that matters to me, I've learned from students (that's another way of again saying I'm using the students' experience as a parable). And as I think about the *separation* between faculty and the many other people engaged in higher education, I am riveted by the subjects of both proximity and motivation. The status quo is well-understood—we periodically reference the "silos" of higher ed with a resigned sigh and then continue with our current habits of interaction. I wonder what it might take for more of us to move from separated strangers to neighbors?

While the class trip to Ecuador required extensive planning, I had another more accidental immersion experience when I won a small grant to buy a one-course release for myself—to start a scholarship of teaching and learning endeavor. That venture included a second office, blocks away from the communication studies department. I moved a few boxes and books across campus to a corner of a slightly remodeled credit union, now dubbed the Faculty Development and Grants Center. Into that small building came faculty of all disciplines, grant-support staff, institutional analysts, and many other assorted colleagues that I hadn't met or talked to during my first few years on campus. This new context produced something akin to culture shock for me—ambiguity and anxiety were a daily norm. Who were these people? What did they do on this campus we shared? How did they get things done? And, why hadn't I been aware of them up until now? That semester of sitting in my corner near the defunct drive-through window and chatting with everyone who came through the door served as the beginning of a period of accelerated motivation to get to know campus neighbors outside my department (no matter how different they seemed). I soon found the soccer game of sorts, as it became apparent that regardless of varied roles and responsibilities, we had shared values—for learning, students, research, and more. I've situated my younger faculty self as a bit ignorant because of isolation, naive to the realities of the broader campus, but I don't think it's an uncommon state for early career faculty. In fact, the *Chronicle of Higher Education* recently posted an article titled "How to Counter the Isolation of Academic Life." In it, authors Trisalyn Nelson and Jessica Early advise that faculty need to actively foster a broad network that includes staff. They describe that network as ". . . an ecology—a living, breathing, ever-shifting collection of connections and contacts that needs time and attention to nurture and grow" (Nelson and Early 2020).

As I help shape this conversation on a snowy Easter in April 2020, the US population has never been more physically separate. It's too early to tell, but perhaps we'll emerge with a renewed motivation to connect.

Bob: One of the blessings of our riffs on the nature of discomforting conversations is that I have come to know you much better—or as you would likely put it, we are now better connected. You are by training as well as instinct, a testifier. Learning for you is tangible, a product of truly getting dirty, sorting the muck of conflict as well as connection. I know I am different. Like you I tell stories, but the lessons drawn are of a different kind. I relish the narrative itself, laying out what happens next and then next and then next again.

Solving the problems we want to address will require both testimony and a detailed analysis yielding new narratives that foster enhanced connections. I suspect you will want to argue that the process necessarily begins with testimony, including the testimony and experiences of the learners our institutions serve. I would have us begin more pragmatically, looking at the behaviors that thwart good conversations and discourage the many from arguing with the few. What we need, frankly, is a process of honest self-examination, which I suspect you will tell me means more testimonies yielding more productive connections.

Perhaps the place to begin is with a frank admission that as faculty we are afraid to talk to one another in the ways you and I have been talking to each other. What is required is a willingness to say out loud that we no longer know how to talk to one another and hence the underlying sense of disconnection. The question my more practical self asks is what would have to happen to start the conversations—not as invitations to a dance, but as the first steps leading to a more permanent change in habits and expectations. My answer is simply, "Do more things together." The problem with silos is that they reinforce the notion that we are on our own. We are not, or at least shouldn't be.

In the 1970s, Whittier College began an interesting experiment with something faculty called paired courses. The idea was that any pair of faculty members from different departments would jointly teach a course that collectively drew on each of their disciplines. Often the pair consisted of someone from the humanities or social sciences paired with someone from the sciences. Another frequent pairing involved a faculty member from a language department co-teaching with almost any other faculty member. Frequently these paired courses involved travel to a country whose native language was other than English. I had long graduated from Whittier by the time the pairs experiment was launched. But one of my closest undergraduate friends had returned to the college as a professor of sociology. Les Howard was by nature a pairs-enthusiast and regularly shared with me how he was managing an experience that nothing in his graduate training had prepared him for. What he got from this experience, beyond cross-disciplinary insights, was a network of friends and colleagues who really knew each other. It was not that much different than sitting in a corner office and purposefully talking with everybody who wandered by.

There were also political benefits that accrued to my friend. He really did know how to get things done in no small part because his continual teaching of different paired courses ultimately made him a nearly indispensable colleague who knew how to have productive conversations.

Lori: What a startlingly simple yet powerful approach to connecting the unconnected, breaking down disciplinary silos while at the same time enhancing outcomes as well as the quality of life for those involved. Now, let's amp that up—let's drop some folks in the jungle, shall we? For example, several college presidents have taken on the role of learner, even writing books about their experiences. Roger Martin is one such president, who dropped himself into the freshman class at St. John's College in Annapolis, Maryland, after surviving a bout with cancer. His memoir, *Racing Odysseus*, is a worthy read (Martin 2010). As you can imagine, many have called him "courageous."

What might such courage look like in a reorganized, connected campus community? On my campus, the academic department is interdisciplinary, designed to ensure rich relationships across traditional divides. What else could be done, beyond the disciplines? Might faculty routinely shadow administrators or residential life directors or graduate students (and vice versa)? Could committees (and the conversation groups we're recommending) habitually include voices of students, staff, alumni, employers, and even parents or families? Yes, we'd be introducing ambiguity and anxiety by not pairing like with like, but the richness we need to revitalize our sector would be well served.

Maybe you're thinking, "That's sweet, Lori. Swell idea, but seriously, not feasible. It's not that I lack courage; I lack time. I can barely keep up with the meetings I have now, and even choosing to be involved in faculty governance is a burden. I think I'll move on to the next chapter." For those who can stay with this line of thinking, know that I'm imagining a dramatically reengineered campus structure, one that values consultation and acknowledges time constraints while also ensuring that we connect those who are currently disconnected. What can you envision for your campus? Faculty leadership. Inclusive decision-making teams. Skilled facilitation. Ongoing listening mechanisms. Data-infused decision making, with relevant "evidence" expected on every agenda. Broad campus awareness of financial realities. Shared principles for risk assessment. Sprints, agility, and more. With a structure that honors connection, not only would we have to change our routines and speed, we'd experience other kinds of disconcerting moments as well. Rumbles would abound. Maybe even those questions that we don't want answers to would be boldly asked. Faculty might have to sit with the discomfort of hearing an employer say that grads are not prepared or listen as students vent about their struggle to afford tuition or to see the relevance of general education courses.

Here's the connection conundrum for faculty. Being an independent contractor (or member of a cozy cadre) may be comfortable, but if you approach your life's work in that way, sequestered from many relevant perspectives, you relinquish the potential to lead and influence.

The campus disconnection phenomenon extends beyond people being segregated into rigid silos. Core to the mission and value-proposition of higher education are our contributions to society through research. Cures, insights, and other discoveries, are vital to human flourishing. Through rigorous methodologies and peer review, we seek to make a difference by producing new knowledge. Again and again, this outcome is realized, to the benefit of many. Once we produce results, we expect those results to impact practice. As the world waits breathlessly for reliable COVID-19 antibody testing and a vaccine, the value of research is perhaps at an all-time high.

What surprises me most about higher education's research mission is the disconnection of research and practice within our own enterprise. When it comes to discerning what works in educational practice, we have results. Though there are still many questions to pursue, much is known about the efficacy of various educational practices. From curriculum structures, to student life programming, to pedagogy, we have produced knowledge that needs to inform practice. Learning cohorts. Writing-intensive courses. First-year seminars. Community-based learning (and much, much more). In a few states, governing boards are requiring that graduates engage in one or two "high-impact practices" to graduate. Many honors programs embed evidence-based approaches for the few, and yet, broadly, such is not the case. As retention and graduation rates for underrepresented populations continue to languish, educational practice on most campuses is not connected to published research. What changes would ensue in your classroom and across your campus if educational research results were intentionally connected to practice, as a baseline expectation? Think of the impact, not only on student outcomes (the most important measure) but also on teaching evaluations, promotions, innovation funds, board reports, grant acceptance, college rankings, and more.

Every disconnection in our enterprise needs inspection. What overt justifications or invisible assumptions protect the division of people and ideas on and across our campuses, and to what end?

Bob: Amen. The problem that frustrates us both is not that we lack ambition but that we are short on sustained successes. I spoke earlier about the pairs program at Whittier College. Alas, today it is an innovation that has almost wholly disappeared. I took advantage of my position as a college trustee—chair of the Academic Affairs Trustee Committee no less—to ask the college's vice president of academic affairs and dean of faculty what happened. He paused and then told me that over the past decade, the pairs program was an unexpected victim of the college's success. Enrollment had nearly doubled. New faculty hires had outstanding research credentials and, being more attuned to their prospects for promotion, were more reluctant to invest the extra time teaching a paired course required. The increase in enrollment had also led to an increase in the hiring of non-tenure-track faculty whose appointments did not allow participation in the pairs program. What was really sad was that the gradual disappearance of the pairs program was proceeding largely unnoticed. Making the kinds of connections the pairs program promised wasn't on enough campus "to-do" lists to sustain a once successful innovation and point of connection.

Our conversation has benefited from a close reading of Randall Bass's article "Disrupting Ourselves: The Problem of Learning in Higher Education." Professor Bass serves as vice president for strategic education initiatives at Georgetown University. His further reflections are now part of our conversation.

Randy Bass: First, thank you so much for the opportunity to join your conversation. A focus on connection is so welcome in the midst of this period of history marked by academic and social disruption, physical distancing, and now a heightened national coming-to-consciousness around unsettled issues of racial justice and systemic inequities. I think of this period in our history as a particularly "dis-integrative era," driven by a vicious cycle of political polarization and digital age filter bubbles and information bias. Taking on the need to foster more internal "connections" within higher education has to be set against this increasingly polarized landscape and the imperative to emphasize integration in an dis-integrative era. Almost a decade ago, I argued that we can't expect our students to learn how to think and act in integrative ways if we are not ourselves more integrated as institutions and modeling that integration as educators (Bass 2012). Indeed, I think the most important argument for enhancing the connections within the academy is the implied relationship between what we do inside our institutions and the kind of impact we want to have on the outside, whether through our interdisciplinary address to the world's greatest challenges or by the kind of graduates—the kind of changemakers—we seek to send into the world.

With that in mind, I'm struck in your conversation that you are not just talking about any connection but a particular kind of connection. The kind of connection that you were seeking from your students by taking them to the Amazon, or by setting up shop to create a space where faculty across the campus could connect with each other, is the kind of connection that takes people out of their comfort zones. It is rooted in a growth mindset that values stretching oneself by understanding the limits, differences, and commonalities that one has with others. Such connections are dispositional, integrative of knowledge and skills, but ultimately grounded in a way of being.

Thought of this way, the disposition to seek such connections, and the capacities to nurture and learn from them, should be among the most important ends or aims of a higher education. My strongest response to your conversation is that we need to make the *capacity to connect* among the most important essential learning outcomes of any higher education degree. I won't take the space here to argue all of the ways that the capacity to connect with other human beings should move up the list of competencies we value. That's a different essay. My point here is simply that there are only two things that get widely valued in higher education: (1) The activities for which people are rewarded. As all rational economic actors do, faculty will prioritize these activities out of self-interest. (2) The learning goals and impacts that we value for our students. Most faculty will prioritize these outcomes out of their dedication to professional practice and their disciplines, and more broadly to society. In the best of circumstances, number 1 aligns with number 2.

So that makes me think about your point, "Do more things together." I reflected on where I have seen those kinds of positive connections among faculty in recent years on my own campus (and I can think of many others elsewhere). One context has been in the organization of large thematic networks of faculty around global challenges (in part, organizing for an upcoming capital campaign). In the "Tech and Society" theme, to take one example, faculty from a huge range of fields—including pure and applied researchers, policy experts, and practitioners—are all connecting to each other at the frontiers of knowledge around data, privacy, artificial intelligence, security, autonomy, ethics, and so forth. And they are doing this in the context of creating new synergies in research, teaching, and the engagement of students.

Similarly, we are in the fourth year of what we call "Core Pathways," a signature experiment in our core curriculum that builds an interlocking set of disciplinary learning experiences around a complex global challenge (the longest running theme being climate change and the environment). We recruited an initial block of a dozen faculty from about seven disciplines to create the first prototype that balanced distinct disciplinary modules with integrated interdisciplinary learning experiences. We provide the scaffolding for the curricular framework, but the faculty community drives each semester's creative approaches and integrative activities across the courses. The rallying cry from the beginning was simply, "If we value interdisciplinary connections and integrative thinking in our students, then how are *we* modeling this for them?" That simple idea has now powered, for several years, one of the most authentically engaged faculty communities I've seen in three decades at my institution.

My takeaway from these two examples is that faculty are eager to connect across silos when their natural self-interest aligns with a greater sense of purpose and aspirations of impact. So, to return to my point above, what if we not only valued such connections as a consequence of focusing on a greater purpose, but valued cultivating a *capacity to connect* as a core outcome of a higher education? What if we sought to name and support the capacity to connect as essential both to healing our world and preparing the next generation to address its existential threats? Increasingly, faculty recognize the value of connections in their own work; could cultivating the disposition to connect be seen as equally valuable? If so, then how could we possibly expect to cultivate that in our students if we weren't modeling it for them?

Lori: Randy has asked questions that penetrate beyond a surface understanding into the heart of the matter. As you convene a campus conversation on the topic of connection, his ending questions may be just what you need to get started: *How can it be that faculty and our current students emerge from their education without having advanced their capacity to connect? If we were designing a campus (or a higher education ecosystem) that included this competence as central, what would it look like?* And, to that end, *How can we more fully integrate scholarship and practice on this campus and beyond?* Having endured extended "distancing" required for public health, your campus colleagues will likely bring fresh eyes and new motivation to this topic—just what is needed for a revitalizing conversation.

Why Are We the Bad Guys?

JOINING THE CONVERSATION: LYNN PASQUERELLA, president, Association of American Colleges and Universities

Bob: We were heroes once: scholars, teachers, experts—professors. My dad, an internist turned psychiatrist in his late forties, really wanted to be a professor, so I became one. It was an intriguing echo of John Adams's boast that he was a soldier (more than a slight exaggeration) so that his son could become a diplomat and his son a professor. In the mid-1950s in America professors were an integral part of the landscape. They had produced the atomic bomb. Were responsible for penicillin. Professors were reorganizing our economy and how, as a culture, we thought about money. In my home we avidly watched *The Halls of Ivy*, telling the stories of a then-modern academic family, starring Ronald Coleman and his equally elegant wife, Benita Hume. It was more than a little unreal—too white, too male, too falsely intellectual—but nonetheless the stuff of an American legend, though the actors were themselves eminently British.

You have to be my age to remember such a time. In short order the Halls were replaced by Richard Burton and Elizabeth Taylor holding forth in *Who's Afraid of Virginia Woolf?* George, a forever associate professor, and Martha, the daughter of the college's president, see their lives and each other as anything but heroic. And it's been pretty much downhill since then. Today we professors are more likely to be portrayed as not just distracted but irrelevant. The right sees us as dangerous ideologues intent on misdirecting the youth of the nation. Activists on the left portray us as not just part of the problem, but the problem itself: old, mostly white men intent on protecting our privileged positions.

The collateral damage from these collective caricatures includes the diminishing of the importance of experts and expertise. Everything is opinion or belief or whatever. In the eyes of too many, professors no longer enjoy a special claim to truth or objectivity. What we teach is not what students want or need but rather what we want and need to honor. Taken together it is a portrait of colleges and universities that are becoming unnecessary. The one silver lining is that on many alumni surveys what respondents still report as remembering most is the great teacher who helped shape their lives.

The notion that we are now the bad guys is a conversation worth having—not so much to explain why, but rather to chart a different future.

Lori: The key to charting that different future is jumping off the page for me, in what you describe as the "one silver lining." As faculty, it is in our *translation* of our expertise through teaching that we really shine as "good" rather than "bad." Expecting to be revered simply because we are the holders of knowledge is not realistic. Rather, what matters is how we communicate our curiosity about a subject and our care for the learner. It is in the potency of the teacher-learner relationship that some among us serve as heroes to our students. Let's be sure to come back to that sliver of silver.

At the same time, if our area of expertise leads us to challenge cultural norms associated with political positions, we have to do so with eyes wide open. Perhaps in the historical period you describe, temporary to be sure, the status associated with the professoriate came from their affiliation with the powerful. Sometimes, from some vantage points, the legitimate expertise emanating from our research situates us as bad guys. Generally, challenging the status quo doesn't lead to standing ovations from the masses. Of course, some of the bad press is justified by poor behavior, but other negative perceptions are based on stereotypes that scapegoat the academe.

A few years ago I was recruiting participants for my research on clergy communication. A large denomination was hosting a national clergy gathering at a local conference center. It seemed like a perfect opportunity to increase the size of my participant pool. The conference center director was a pal who arranged for me to provide a quick announcement at the conclusion of a keynote address. I slipped in the back of the auditorium near the end of session, noticing I was the only woman in the room. As I listened to the closing, I quickly discerned the speaker's theme: Here's How to Inoculate College-Bound Young People in Your Church against the Evil Professors at Public Universities. And yes, the word "evil" was actually spoken, not implied. So, when he was done and the applause subsided, I got my cue to go to the front of the room to provide my chipper public service announcement. I started with a warm smile. "Hi!" I said. "I'm Lori, a public university professor." The room got rather quiet, and I hoped my presence and research focus created some memorable dissonance for attendees. Let's notice though—this circumstance was unusual. How often does our research lead us to direct interaction with those who think we are the enemy? Perhaps we're as separated today from some groups and perspectives as the elite were set apart in the heyday of academic heroism that you described. I'm wondering how we can intentionally place ourselves in conversation with those who don't value the work we do, particularly in research? I'm also wondering if we have the capacity and motivation to engage in the public discourse in ways that shift the narrative. While students who sign up for our classes situate themselves with some degree of vulnerability as learners, others outside our classrooms and context aren't necessarily open to what we have to offer. One thing is for sure: simply "being an expert" will not change perceptions, even if we cry foul.

We academics do differ from the norm now. As a group, we remain steadfastly committed to evidence, data, and science to make decisions, while others do not. The Pew Research Center's many investigations yield now-familiar descriptions of the current state:

> In the U.S. and abroad, anxiety over misinformation has increased alongside political polarization and growing fragmentation of the media. Faith in expertise and institutions has declined, cynicism has risen, and citizens are becoming their own information curators. All of these trends are fundamentally changing the way people arrive at the kind of informed opinions that can drive effective governance and political compromise. . . .
>
> Many Americans tell us that when making important decisions, they "do their own research" rather than trust expert advice. But most of that research still involves deciding which information to trust and what to ignore. And as a growing share of Americans depend on mobile devices for the vast majority of their digital engagement, the nature of that engagement continues to evolve. (Dimock 2019)

While the preponderance of evidence in the two-thousand teens led to these kinds of conclusions, the new decade has started memorably. In the current public health crisis of 2020, dependence on expertise is surging, as is the stark need for research and discovery.

Bob: You have surprised me once again. I don't think the problem is our adherence as scholars to evidence-based research but rather our discovery that what we believe in no longer matters as much as we want it to. It is a worry that has made us unexpectedly defensive.

Ironically, it is our teaching that gets us into the most trouble. The old caricature of the professor who proudly proclaims, "I don't teach students, I teach chemistry!" is too close to the mark for comfort—and the phrase could as easily have been, "I don't teach students, I teach Shakespeare!" I have said this before, but it bears repeating: as faculty we don't teach what students need or want but rather what we want to teach and need to honor. And we have been found out. Almost no one is fooled by our insistence that how and what we teach is preordained.

I have spent much of the past twenty years arguing that we need to rethink—or rather discard and replace—the standard undergraduate curriculum with something that works, not for us, but for our students. We need to stop teaching as we were taught, and teach instead as if we understood our students and the kinds of knowledge and habits of mind that will serve them best in a truly turbulent world. If we want to stop being the bad guys, we need to admit we've often been mistaken and change our behavior accordingly.

Which brings me to Anthony Wallace and his notion of revitalization. When I joined the Penn faculty, Wallace's reputation as an anthropologist and social theorist was anchoring an anthropology department that was already considered one of Penn's crown jewels. While his interests and writings were wide ranging, much of Wallace's importance then as now was attributed to his breakout paper, "Revitalization Movements," published in 1956. Wallace was interested in how cultures, particularly those that are atrophying, can develop the capacity to change themselves. That process Wallace defined as a revitalization movement. And like you, Lori, he framed his theory with personal testimony in his book *Religion: An Anthropological View*: "When I was in my teens, I visited the Iroquois reservation at Grand River in Ontario with my father, who was interested in the leaders of the Handsome Lake religion and in the League of the Iroquois. That experience, together with early studies of Teedyuscung, an eighteenth-century Delaware Indian convert to the Moravian faith, led me to the study of the Handsome Lake religion, from which my more general interests grew" (Wallace 1966). The subject of Wallace's ruminations about the restoration of the Seneca Nation to its former glory was the story of Handsome Lake, a Seneca chief who had fallen on hard times:

> Handsome Lake's personal difficulties mirrored the tribulations of Iroquois society. In two generations the Iroquois had fallen from high estate to low. . . . They had seen their towns burned, their people dispersed, and, after the American Revolution, their statesmen and warriors made to seem contemptible because they had supported the losing side. They had lost their lands and were confined to a sprinkling of tiny reservations, slums in the wilderness, lonely islands of aboriginal tradition scattered among burgeoning white settlements. They faced a moral crisis: they wanted still to be men

and women of dignity, but they knew only the old ways, which no longer led to honor . . . but only to poverty; to abandon these old ways meant undertaking customs that were strange, in some matters repugnant, and in any case uncertain of success. . . .

Into this moral chaos, Handsome Lake's revelations of the word of God sped like a golden arrow, dispelling darkness and gloom. Heavenly messengers, he said, had told him that unless he and his fellows became new men, they were doomed to be destroyed in an apocalyptic world destruction. . . . Handsome Lake went on, in detailed vision after vision, to describe the sins that afflicted the Iroquois of 1799 and to prescribe the new way of life that would avert the fiery judgment. Some of his instructions were directed toward theological and ritual matters, but the bulk of his code was directed toward the resolution of moral issues presented by the new social and economic situation of the reservation Iroquois. . . . He told the Iroquois to adopt the white man's mode of agriculture. (Wallace 1966)

Wallace went on to formalize his concept of revitalization, outlining distinct stages and consequences. Each of the stages are important, though for the most part, they lie outside the scope of our conversation here. The exception is revitalization's fifth stage: communication:

The aim of the communication is to make converts. The code is offered as the means of spiritual salvation for the individual and of cultural salvation for the society. Benefits promised to the target population need not be immediate or materialistic, for the basis of the code's appeal is the attractiveness of identification with a more highly organized system, with all that this implies in the way of self-respect. Indeed, in view of the extensiveness of the changes in values, promises of material and social benefits meaningful in the old system would often be pointless. Religious codes offer spiritual salvation, identification with God, elect status; political codes offer honor, fame, the respect of society for sacrifices made in its interest. Refusal to accept the code, on the other hand, is usually defined as placing the listener in immediate spiritual, as well as material, peril with respect to his existing values as well as new ones. In small societies, the target population may be the entire community; but in more complex societies, the message may be aimed only at certain groups deemed eligible for participation in the transfer and goal cultures. (Wallace 1966)

Wallace's recounting his coming to understand the process of cultural revitalization, reminds me of Gawande's telling of the story (in conversation 1) of the revitalization of a nursing home culture in the twentieth century. I understand Wallace's and Gawande's differences—different eras, ethnicities, and disciplines, while the latter is principally a doer; the former, an observer and theoretician—but what they share is more important. Both are concerned with communities in general and in particular with community cultures in decline.

Each is a masterful storyteller. Each describes actions that changed the rules, though breaking the rules may prove a more apt description. Each conceives of change processes that harness the energies of communities that had hitherto been thwarted. And each sees communication—verbal and symbolic—as the key to transforming cultures of acquiescence into cultures of action. Wallace also understands that eventually revitalized communities will produce bureaucracies of their own that in time will necessarily become ripe for revitalization. Though they don't use the same terms, Gawande is writing about a community being revitalized, and Wallace is writing about the importance of purposeful living.

There is nothing that is subtle in my linking the stories these two scholars told. What we as faculty need to do to become good guys again is to revitalize our academic communities, and that requires changing not just our assumptions and predilections, but just as important, our behavior as well. We don't need a shaman or prophet imbued with supernatural powers, but we do need articulate leaders who can say—as Handsome Lake regularly said—we have lost our way and need to change.

Lori: Such an admission needs a motivational catalyst—a crisis, a startling realization brought on by reflection, an experience of awakening. We are suggesting that conversations can serve that function, provided we don't simply talk with those with whom we already see eye to eye. What is essential in your conclusion here is the recognition of who needs to do the changing if revitalization is to occur. It is us. For the tired, the committed— the discouraged, and the well-intentioned—that is a tough admission.

Early in my career as an educator, I left a teaching job in my hometown high school in Indiana for an adventure in a Yup'ik Eskimo village school in the bush of Alaska. My aim was altruistic, to be sure. I naively imagined myself making a difference in the world by teaching in such a remote place. The district provided a two-hour in-service training session before I was flown 500 miles west of Anchorage, landing in a bush plane on a narrow strip of tundra. In the first snowy weeks in that village, I had one of those conversations that ultimately led to an awakening.

I was seated next to a teenage boy named Apaq. We were looking at the screen of an Apple IIE, trying to get to an English lesson I had assigned. As I struggled with the floppy disk, I could feel Apaq staring at me. Nothing in the in-service or my (limited!) prior experience had prepared me to provide a culturally appropriate response to the stare of a young Eskimo, so I just blurted out, "Apaq, what are you staring at?"

He leaned in even closer and asked, "What you see when you look out?"

"What?" I said. "I see the computer, the classroom, the snow out the window. What do you mean, what do I see?"

Then, to my dismay, he leaned in closer still. Now nearly nose to nose he asked me quietly, "It all blue?"

Apaq had never been that close to a blue-eyed person before. I laughed and assured him that when I looked out and he looked out, we saw exactly the same world. But—oh—was I wrong. Of course, it wasn't the color of our eyes that determined that difference in our views, but rather our cultures, histories, language, roles, and more. My ignorance, coupled with my positive intent, made for a dangerous combination. Thankfully, my Yup'ik students were great teachers.

When I presented lessons deductively, with bulletin boards that matched my learning outcomes and lovely little note-taking guides that would have received gold stars in my Hoosier hometown, Apaq and his classmates said, "You make no sense."

When I approached instruction in an animated way, they said, "So embarrassing."

And when, schooled in the Socratic method, I asked questions to generate classroom dialogue, they commented, "So nosy."

And then, a student-confidant (now nurse, grandmother, and Facebook friend), shared the translation of the nickname Apaq and others were calling me—the ugliest of the ugly. Given the standard of beauty in Yup'ik culture, descriptions of my colored eyes, big hair, and beaver teeth gave credence to the nickname—and illustrated well that I did not yet see through the lens of my learners; in fact, I think it would be appropriate to characterize me as nearly blind to their perspectives.

Add to the cultural differences other contextual factors, which included a history of boarding schools, Yup'ik nation sovereignty, the new (state-funded) school building, mandatory attendance, an ethnocentric curriculum, the young teaching squad shipped in from the lower 48, and more. In spite of my years of training and positive intent, I was definitely not a "good guy" in this environment. I was part of a system that assumed it knew what was best without deep listening or adaptation to the actual learners. I was understood to be the stranger who didn't know squat about how things really were—a nice stranger, presumably, but most certainly not a revered or valued expert who understood what the learners were experiencing or what would serve the context or their futures well.

If I was ever going to teach anything to Apaq and his peers, I had to first learn to see—or at least glimpse—through his lens. I had to ask, "What do *you* see when you look out?" and then, listen deeply to the answer, accepting the perspective of the other as not right, not wrong—but real. As educators, as scholars—it is our responsibility to continuously ask that question, humbly, and analytically—and then to use the emerging answers to adapt what and how we teach, and even what we investigate as scholars, and how we share those results. If we seek revitalization, that humble listening in which we set aside judgment of those with whom we differ, is mandatory.

Other conversations in this collection ask us to go deeper still, to change the curriculum, to know our students. But first we need to commit to a process of discovery in which we come to see through the lens of the other, even when we disagree or simply do not understand. It is in meeting learners where they are that we can be our very best, good rather than bad perhaps—but more important, influencers rather than superfluous strangers, contributing to the common good with relevant investment of all we have to offer.

Bob: The trouble with following you in these conversations is that we often talk on parallel tracks, which, if I understand your story, you did with Apaq. And, as has proved so often the case, we have arrived at parallel answers that nonetheless reinforce one another. You are telling our faculty colleagues to ask not just their students but one another, "What do you see when you look out?" Less charitably, I am suggesting that doing what you propose will lead to first an understanding and then to a public acknowledgment that they have at times been wrong, really wrong. It is a feeling that in itself ought to lead to a revitalization movement that is truly revolutionary. You know me well. I am not a pie-eyed optimist. We can become the good guys again, but it will take more than a dash of humility.

In 2016, Lynn Pasquerella followed Carol Geary Schneider as president of the Association of American Colleges and Universities. She brought to the task a fine-tuned sense of academic faculty and now joins our conversation.

Lynn Pasquerella: At a time when there has been a decoupling of higher education from the American Dream, redressing the growing skepticism regarding the value of higher education while destabilizing cultural attitudes that position liberal education as a self-indulgent luxury will require colleges and universities to demonstrate that they are teaching students twenty-first-century skills, within the context of the workforce, not apart from it. A liberal education for the twenty-first century mandates the acceleration of high-impact learning opportunities centered on learning outcomes (knowledge of human cultures and the physical and natural world, intellectual and practical skills, personal and social responsibility, integrative and applied learning) as necessary for all students' intellectual, civic, personal, and professional development, and for success in a global economy. Assignments should make clear the relationships among areas of knowledge, ensuring that students do not see academic disciplines as separate and disconnected silos of learning but rather as varied approaches to the same enlightened end.

In this model, disciplinary work remains foundational, but students are provided with faculty-guided practice connecting their disciplines with others, with the co-curriculum, and with the needs of society, across the curriculum, from their first-to final-semester. Developing this type of deeper-level understanding across subject areas, connecting knowledge to experience, and adopting a holistic approach to evidence-based problem solving that incorporates diverse, sometimes contradictory points of view, is more important than ever in preparing students for success in grappling with the unscripted problems of the future, and for democracy.

Moreover, if we hope to bolster the reputation of higher education, colleges and universities must recommit to serving as anchor institutions, demonstrating that their success is inextricably linked to the physical, psycho-social, and economic well-being of those in the communities in which they are located. This will require transitioning away from the "expert" model of knowledge generation to publicly active scholarship, which enacts democratic engagement designed to promote a more equitable society by partnering with K through 12, business, industry, and citizens themselves by taking advantage of local epistemologies.

Unfortunately, we are at a point in our history when the professional structures of academic scholarship, with its tendency to neglect teaching excellence, outreach, civic engagement, and public intellectualism, continue to marginalize the critical work of those dedicated to providing the broadest access to higher education through humanistic practice. It is time for us to step outside of our echo chambers, move beyond our own language game, and insert ourselves into the public discourse and debates over public policy, collectively reaffirming the role that a liberal education plays in discerning the truth; the ways in which it serves as a catalyst for interrogating the sources of narratives, including history, evidence, and facts; the ways in which a liberal education promotes an understanding that the world is a collection of interdependent yet inequitable systems; the ways in which it expands knowledge of human interactions, privilege, and stratification; and the ways in which higher education fosters equity and justice, locally and globally. Until we change both the curricula and the reward systems within the academy, structural impediments will continue to exacerbate the burgeoning economic segregation in higher education and further erode the concept of higher education as a public good.

Lori: When I hear Lynn's contribution to this conversation, I am struck by the many disjointed pieces of academic life she asks us to connect if we are to avoid being framed as less valuable than we think fair. How ironic that our call for connection in the previous conversation resurfaces as a potent antidote to what ails our collective reputation. As you launch a campus conversation on this topic, I'm hopeful you and your colleagues won't get mired too long in venting about how public perceptions don't square with your good intentions and legitimate contributions (maybe you can set a timer). Instead, let's set aside defensiveness to interrogate reality, asking: *How might the current negative framing of academics impede our efforts to transform higher education, and what can we do about it, as individuals, as a campus community, and as a sector?*

· conversation 6

Money Talks

JOINING THE CONVERSATION: WILLIAM F. MASSY, former chief financial officer and professor emeritus, Stanford University

Bob: I want to return to what we learned from the nearly 200 faculty members whose stories we collected as part of our college curriculum project. The big takeaway was that college communities in general and faculty in particular are ready, willing, and able to change how students are taught, but are neither ready nor able to change the curriculum that governs what their students are taught. The issue was, I have suggested, a matter of the missing "we" in higher education that makes truly collective decisions nearly impossible. Almost as debilitating is higher education's inability to have fruitful discussions about the intertwining of money and unintended consequences. In *Making Sense of the College Curriculum* we told the story of a midwestern college that, having finally succeeded in adopting a new curriculum, discovered it did not have the funds necessary to implement the changes it had agreed to. As it turned out, it was one of several stories related to us by faculty testifying about how good ideas often came a cropper because no one really understood their institution's finances.

Lori: The answer we collected most often as to why institutional finances proved so problematic was that neither the faculty nor the administration knew what their education programs cost. Here's how *Making Sense of the College Curriculum* summed up the problem:

> Too many faculty are not just unprepared but, in fact, are too often reluctant to talk about the costs and financial constraints that impact how they lead their academic lives. We were struck by how seldom the conversations we recorded talked about money or the role money played in the reform process. And often those who did talk about financial constraints were from disciplinary clusters experiencing shortfalls in either general enrollments or their major or, as was most often the case, both. The elements of what we have come to call the cost conundrum reveal themselves in a variety of ways. There are departments or whole institutions that hover near the point of unsustainability, and their faculty express the anxiety this awareness creates, sometimes yielding actions to sustain enrollment that do not sit well from the standpoint of fidelity to the discipline or to students' learning needs. Another manifestation of the conundrum is to be part of a college or department that has increased in enrollment but has not actually increased net tuition revenue; in such cases faculty may find themselves being required to teach more students with the same number of faculty. Sometimes a smaller campus that adopts a curriculum revision to increase learning and save costs realizes it simply lacks the economy of scale to deliver a revised program effectively. Others face the paradox of unforeseen consequences when adopting technology as a way to teach more students efficiently. (Zemsky, Wegner, and Duffield 2018)

Bob: We also collected the story of a physicist whose exasperation with how his institution spent money centered on the particular role student choice played in the process. Drawing on his experience as both a senior member of the faculty and a college administrator he observed:

> One of the things that I began to understand as I did administrative work is that we actually allow students to dictate where we spend money. Where the students go, the money flows. You want students to go to STEM? Instead of

allowing 780 majors in kinesiology here, cut it down to 400. Instead of having 875 business majors, cut it down to 500. Hire faculty, put up a building that has more classrooms, and what a shock: You'll have students majoring in STEM. It's even worse in our local community because in addition to STEM, we've got serious problems with anything related to social issues. Medical, we've got no health professionals in our area. We've got a lot of things we could really address, but it would take somebody who would really have to stir up a pot, right? I mean, because faculty have it in their heads that the way you get more money and make your department bigger and more important is to have more majors. That's just backwards. We are a state university funded by state funding and we need to be able to deliver the goods in terms of having people who are needed to make our state function well. And don't think those departments don't have to change. I mean the physics department would, for example, have to understand that it needs to become more welcoming; so don't get me wrong, it's not just one-sided. It just seems to me wrong from an administrative point of view to run a tax-driven place and let the students decide where the money gets spent. That's just backwards. (Zemsky, Wegner, and Duffield 2018)

At this point we asked Bill Massy to join the conversation, reflecting on his experience as higher education's preeminent model builder and my colleague in a host of projects seeking to make institutional budget and resource policies rational.

Bill Massy: Let me start by observing that it is wrong, in both practice and principle, to leave to students the determination as to where money is spent. The goal in a nonprofit college or university is to further the institution's mission subject to market and financial constraints. Here the term *mission* includes the content and quality of student learning and also the disciplinary values that faculty care about so deeply. It should drive the university's actions to the extent permitted by markets and money. Student preferences reflect market forces. Responding to these forces is very important, but to make this the overarching goal is to confuse not-for-profit universities with profit-making ones. Business firms balance market forces against profitability, with an eye to maximizing financial returns to shareholders. A university doesn't pursue markets or profitability as ends in themselves but rather as means for furthering its mission. In *Reengineering the University* I describe the difference between a university's value proposition as determined by its mission and the value proposition seen by its students. The two propositions must be compatible enough for the institution to succeed in the marketplace, but it's wrong to say that student preferences should be the main driver of university spending. Bob and I have said that universities should be "mission centered, market smart, and margin conscious," and that means making mission-driven decisions as described above.

Bob: I understand your appeal to principle, but I am not sure it is a commitment to being market smart and mission centered that explains why most of the talk about money and its importance is as nonproductive as it is loud. The calmest laments are merely adversarial—the more excited are actually bestial. People see enemies everywhere. They think those with whom they disagree are not just wrong-headed but maliciously as well as fundamentally wrong. Almost everywhere faculty will tell you that the answer to the question, "why is your institution incurring a deficit?" lies with "them, not us," meaning the increasing number of administrative staff and other ancillaries. Or that the administration has the wrong priorities. Or again, because times are against us, we just have to be patient while we wait for the financial picture to change.

The problem is most apparent on campuses with collective bargaining agreements. In the annual or biennial run-up to a new contract there are few if any limits governing what the combatants may claim. In the absence of any give-and-take, there is only loud broadcasting of predetermined bargaining positions. In this regard, academic unions sound no different than the industrial unions that have traditionally held sway in the rest of the economy.

Lori: I think what we have are two often entwined versions of "money talks" in a context that further confuses the overall situation. The most prevalent approach includes shouting matches where blame is parceled out in big loud packages. While the protagonists shout, most of the members of the community look the other way, choosing to go about their business quietly if not in actual silence. The other kind of talk is equally quarrelsome. Here again, most members of the community are not engaged other than to support the general notion that they work too hard for too little money. Taken together, these two perspectives can produce an environment in which there is neither sufficient goodwill nor sufficient technical understanding to promote informed discussion. In the meantime, faculty are largely rendered mute when asked by a friend or neighbor, "Why does a college education have to cost so much?"

Bob: Let me start with a story about what faculty know and don't know about the role money plays on their campuses. A Western-style university in Singapore had asked Bill Massy and me to help frame a discussion focusing on adopting an alternative budget system. Part of our task was to introduce the campus to the mysteries of Responsibility Center Management. We began by spending time with the dean of each college in hopes of allaying any fear that an RCM budget system, in particular, was meant to disadvantage them or their college. Among the deans assigned to me was the one responsible for the college of arts and letters. To say he was nervous is an understatement, and some 50 minutes into our scheduled time together he finally blurted out why he was so uncomfortable—he just knew that we would find that his college was a financial loser. A month later I had sufficient data with which to recast his college's budget using the rules and terms of responsibility budgeting: his college was credited with all its own revenues, charged with all its own expenses plus a proportional share of the expenses associated with the university's central administrative services. What we learned, to our amazement, was that the college of arts and letters was in fact a cash cow, supplying significant surpluses to be spent elsewhere in the university. Why? Because the college had all those required first-year general education courses that were remarkably cheap to teach. While the dean understood the financial importance of first-year enrollments, what he was missing was an understanding of how the surpluses those courses generated were being spent elsewhere by others. What he needed was some careful instruction as to how we determined a college's bottom line using the rules of responsibility center management. And even then he wasn't sure that his colleagues across the university would draw the same lessons from the data that Bill and I drew. The idea that arts and letters was a financial loser was stitched deeply into the university's DNA.

Lori: Fogginess regarding the flow of tuition and other revenue is a significant part of the challenge, to be sure. Though you may think I'm going on a tangent, the story raises a red flag for me. Why are first-year, gen ed courses cheap? I see a lecture pit, students memorizing soon-to-be forgotten tidbits of information because their course grade is based on a few multiple-choice exams, an underpaid TA, and high DFW (D, fail, or withdraw) rates. The "cost" of this traditional approach is substantial and cannot be forgotten as we talk about money. Curricular and pedagogical changes could increase student success in such courses, decreasing the loss of tuition revenue from students who drop out (not to mention the human potential that is squandered). DFW rates in gateway courses like these negatively impact retention and time to degree, and those impacts are experienced disproportionately by underrepresented populations. Dropping out with student debt is a worst-case scenario, with costs to individuals, the economy, and the public perception of higher education.

Perhaps I've started preaching and need to stop until we get to some of the other conversation topics, but you know I'm an advocate for investing in the *quality* of teaching and learning, requiring tough decisions about what else in the university might have to be cut to make those learner-centered decisions. As we generate dialogue about unit budget allocation, tuition, other revenue flow on campus, and expenditure authority, let's just not forget that the whole enterprise needs to change.

Bob: What I am talking about is that productive discussions about money require substantial technical knowledge along with a climate of trust. Of course, conversations about teaching and learning similarly require substantive expertise. Just shouting out well-worn catch phrases will not suffice. We will need to return to this issue when we talk about the kind of conversations on which curricular reform is dependent.

Lori: I look forward to diving into that one. Sometimes we educators hear the words "cost-saving measures" and "efficiency" as euphemisms for implementing practices that will decrease the quality of education. Whatever we choose to do to address financial realities, keeping mission at the center is absolutely vital.

Bill Massy: I, too, have encountered faculty concerns that "cost saving" and "efficiency" are euphemisms for quality degradation and increased work for faculty. Yet, circumstances arise where the institution has no choice but to bring its costs into line with revenues. The irony is that, when faculty don't actively participate in such efforts, they dramatically increase the likelihood of quality degradation and increased workloads—the very things the school needs to defend. Good administrators do care about these problems, but they can't address them without active faculty participation. The reason is simple: God is in the details when it comes to cost saving and efficiency improvement, and even experienced academic leaders can't possibly know enough to get things right without the involvement of currently serving faculty. Administrators should try hard to improve efficiency in overhead areas before looking at the academic ones, but in today's environment that's unlikely to suffice. Academic-economic trade-offs involving the size of majors and the proliferation of courses, for example, have to be confronted. Deciding "by the numbers" (for example, class sizes and departmental margins) essentially guarantees inferior results.

Bob: What our collection of faculty experiences revealed was that almost no one outside the comptroller's shop had a functioning understanding of their institution's economy—and that understanding was invariably presented in terms derived from the institution's audited financial reports, which very few had actually seen and even fewer understood. Ask faculty members, as our project did, what they knew about how their institution's allocated funds, nearly every answer referenced first and foremost "butts in seats." All that really mattered was how many students a faculty member was credited with teaching.

Lori: Bob, your stories are as familiar as they are painful. If we can stand it, I need to pile on a bit. In many public university systems state funding continues a steep decline. I know that last sentence is not a surprise to anyone, but the experience this reality creates for thousands of educators needs further conversation. In the regional comprehensives, resource infusion from philanthropy and large grant procurement generally is much less substantial than at the "flagship" institutions, in part because regional campuses provide high levels of access and outreach expected by the land-grant mission. Those commitments can be consuming.

In the past decade, many faculty saw increases in their class sizes and health premiums, while even the highest merit-based annual salary increase didn't keep pace with the cost of living. As I'm sure is true elsewhere, I witnessed Wisconsin faculty staying committed to their students and campuses because at least for a time, the external forces seemed miles away from the compelling daily activities of learning and teaching. At the same time, internal resources to drive new initiatives were hard to come by. As the director of a teaching and learning center, I heard many versions of this kind of question from devoted faculty: *How do we take the time to collaborate so we can enact research-based practice when there are more papers than ever to grade and the research expectations we have for ourselves are not diminishing?* In these environments where the amount of both time and money is shrinking, a shared identity as "victims" often develops, exacerbated by negative public rhetoric that is echoed (and sometimes even championed) by governing boards and other state leaders. If the faculty is unionized and contract negotiations are prolonged, a "work to rule" habit of investing at a baseline level can even ensue. Just when it seems things can't get worse, a social media rant about the salary of the football coach at the flagship will go viral, and the daily lives of faculty and student development staff may feel even more meager.

Bob: And what of administrators?

Lori: Well, former faculty turned deans, provosts, and presidents are desperately looking for sweeping strategies to increase resources or diminish expenses while sharing the real and positive stories of student success that keep everyone motivated. "They think I have a honey pot in my office," said one president of a community college in the Deep South. On that campus with high teaching loads, students who complete their degrees are literally lifted out of poverty. With such compelling outcomes, the lack of money to innovate or even operate creates dissonance and sometimes suspicion. Even with a unifying mission like that, a "lack of transparency" by administrators can be assumed by staff and faculty, especially if realistic "money talks" are not routine.

Bob, you called it right—generally, the professional educators living out the higher ed mission do not know the basics about the finances of their enterprise. That's not part of the orientation. As a young faculty member, I was enthused to propose a new course in "Intercultural Communication." My rationale was solid, if not inspirational. Students would benefit from this course—no doubt about it. As a more experienced colleague guided me through the completion of the lengthy "New Course Proposal Form," I came across the item "new resources required." "Oh," she said, "don't check that box or it will never be approved." That was the extent of our thinking about the budget implications of my good idea. Later, as I began my gradual slide into administration, I learned that hundreds of courses had been added over the years while very few had been removed. Still later in my journey, I watched an opening day assembly of faculty and staff shocked into silence as a trusted new dean from the mathematics department shared that 99 percent of the college's allocated budget for the year was already committed to salaries and fringe benefits. Keeping costs invisible to practitioners has been standard procedure on many campuses, a habit that is counterproductive to generating either a trusting community or collective innovation. This reality of finite and shrinking resources needs our ongoing mutual discussion if new ways of being are to emerge.

Bob: In campus contexts where conflicts about financial constraints have become debilitating, it might be hard to imagine such conversations, but we both know they can happen. You just told a story about a classic conflict over class size and teaching loads.

Lori: Yes, in that case, an academic leader started by asking faculty in specific disciplines (writing, math, etc.) to determine the maximum class sizes for effective learning in core courses. Using their conclusions to frame a financial discussion, she revealed the cost of running courses that were short on students. A clear chart showing the impact of class size on instructional costs was given to faculty—the first time many had seen the basic figures. Ultimately, upon review and with extensive deliberation, they were convinced by the data. On that campus thousands of dollars have now been saved by running courses at faculty-determined capacities, with the savings invested in other initiatives to fuel student success. The administrator set the table for this transformation by showing respect for faculty judgment, knowing that their course capacity conclusions emanated from a deep commitment to student learning—one that she shared.

Bob: What you need first is a true conversation that establishes trust. In your example you make the charts self-evident. It seldom works out that way. I have spent a lifetime presenting what I thought were perfectly clear charts to faculty committees only to discover that "perfectly clear" was in the eye of the beholder. What was needed as you know well was a commitment to trust on the part of everyone in the room before anyone showed anybody a chart or graph or even a single number.

Lori: Assuming the positive intent of one's conversation partner is a basic for constructive communication. So here we are in the conversation that's supposed to be about finance and we're back to the topic of trust. I remember learning about the "helical" model of communication. You can imagine the shape, but the point was that an interaction that happened 20 years ago could impact how your "perfectly clear chart" was interpreted by the faculty committee. For example, in one history department such a chart had once been used in an administrative effort that led to the dismissal of tenured faculty. Now, a couple of decades later, the chart itself gets resurrected routinely as the symbol to justify mistrust of new administrative initiatives.

Bob: The answer, I think, is simpler than you imagine but ultimately more difficult to realize. For a real conversation about money to proceed, there has to be general agreement that "history starts now." No going back and rearguing the past. Faculty are particularly wary of making such a concession because we are inordinately fond of precedent.

Lori: Right. And that's a crucial element of what needs to change. In some cases, apologies or at least an airing of that history is necessary. Direct confrontation of the unspeakables is imperative. The principles of restorative justice may be useful to all involved. That's not easy to do, but a blanket declaration that we're starting fresh is also tough, unless a leader has generated such deep personal trust and credibility that the faculty are willing to move on because that leader symbolizes an absolutely new day.

Bob: Fair enough, but now it is time to turn to the toughest problem facing those who believe that talking about money is not only possible but helpful. What literally no one on the faculty wants to talk about is that our institutions have in fact become less efficient and hence more expensive. Indeed the upward drift in expenses derives in large part from an ingrained faculty habit of always adding but almost never subtracting. It's the forgotten lesson at the heart of University of Iowa president Howard Bowen's oft-quoted observation, "Universities will raise all the money they can and will spend all the money they raise because there are so many good things to spend their money on" (Bowen 1980). It is the dangling tag line that is the key. Too many good ideas coupled with never sufficient discipline to limit the academy's appetites.

Lori: Agreed, but don't forget that the sort of "discipline" you reference is not the responsibility of any one faculty member but instead requires the kind of cross-campus as well as interdisciplinary conversations that need to become a routine part of campus life. Even now, as we approach a fall 2020 semester in the context of the pandemic, on some campuses individual faculty members have been granted the right to determine the modality of the courses they teach. This humane approach to an evolving situation also illuminates the intersections and collective impact of their independent decisions. Ultimately, course modality choices may have financial implications for the campus as a whole. It's a time of high anxiety, to be sure, one in which the reality check of a campuswide money talk has never been more necessary.

Bob: There are lots of examples that make this point, but the most poignant almost always involve the curriculum and the growth in the number of majors. My favorite involves a midwestern liberal arts college that once had 1,500 students but was now struggling with just 900. To attract more students it had added more majors, so that at the time of my visit the college was offering 67 separate majors. The real problem, however, was that just 4 of those majors absorbed 60 percent of all enrollments, leaving 360 students to be spread across 63 majors, or roughly 5.7 students per major. Even once it became clear that increasing the number of majors to yield more enrollees wasn't working, the habit of adding more and subtracting none held sway. And make no mistake, there are plenty of colleges with stable enrollments that have increased the number of individual majors they offer as a means of preserving current revenue. Inevitably, the result has been the same: at best a modest increase in revenue offset by an increase in costs derived from a curriculum that is both more awkward and less efficient.

Lori: And though we'll be talking more about curriculum next, I have to interrupt with a reminder that the very idea of a "major" needs our collective inquiry, in addition to the financial implications of adding majors as a marketing mechanism to attract additional new students and their tuition dollars.

Bob: To begin, what is required is an informed, faculty-driven conversation yielding a practical understanding of how the habit of adding but not subtracting is defining a future for American higher education that is not sustainable. The ability to convene and then conclude such conversations—and yes, that includes an understanding of how best to reduce the size of the current faculty in order to fund future faculty additions—is an operational imperative. What won't work is a further hunkering down that reinforces an understanding of institutional finances that focuses on nothing more than butts in seats.

Lori: And while these conversations can accomplish a much-needed setting of realistic expectations, given faculty facilitation these dialogues could also generate creative new approaches to curriculum and pedagogy that are both learner-centered and fiscally responsible.

Bill Massy: Sound and relevant data are a prerequisite for informed, faculty-driven conversations. Such data couldn't be provided until recently, and faculty are right to be skeptical about the data that have typically been offered. Even the best-intentioned efforts to achieve transparency fail when the data ignore, or consider superficially, too many things that the faculty know to be important. Happily, a new breed of academic resourcing models can provide data that faculty find to be genuinely useful. The models extract information about individual courses from the university's scheduling, student registration, and other systems. They support the whole range of academic resourcing decisions: from setting the roster and configuration of courses offered by departments, to balancing the university's portfolio of degree and certificate programs, to the addition or elimination of faculty lines in budget determination. I describe the new breed of models, and the ways in which they are being used by institutions, in my *Resource Management for Colleges and Universities* (Massy 2020). It's my fervent hope that these models will mitigate the mistrust that bedevils many academic resourcing conversations, so that the conversations described in this chapter can proceed effectively.

Bob: At this point we need to make an important shift in what I like to call our "conversation strategy." In each of our first conversations we called for a general, everybody-in conversation. Quite literally, the more the better. Conversations about money need to be different—more organized, more disciplined, more committed to making a decision, no matter how politically risky such a commitment might prove.

When it comes to money, what is needed is really strong presidential leadership, shaped through ongoing conversations with trustees. Start with a board-endorsed announcement that the time to reengineer the budget is finally at hand. What is needed is not just a commitment to reducing costs but a successful strategy for getting the job done now, before the end of the current academic year. To that end the president announces the appointment of a task force that will meet continually over the course of the year before announcing the consensus that will bring the task to completion by a clear deadline.

The trick is to commit in advance to make the difficult decisions and to back up that commitment by entrusting the process to a group of true campus citizens, mostly, but not exclusively members of the faculty. The leader of the process must necessarily be a facilitator "extraordinaire." The process begins with a pure exploration, a "trying on" of all the difficult, nearly impossible conversations we have identified. Week by week the task force teaches itself the dynamics of the budget, including exactly why a "reengineered budget" is a necessity. Why, to put the matter more bluntly, the campus needs to spend money differently so that it can spend its money more efficiently. Come January, specific adjustments must be considered, if at all possible, within the confidence of the task force. Assuming the task force achieves a basic consensus, the last two months of the task force's life needs to be devoted to organizing a campaign—quite literally something akin to a political campaign—extending the task force's conversation to the entire campus community. Here the trick is to remain committed to reengineering. Putting the necessary decisions off to a later day is not an acceptable ploy.

What do you think? Could such a forced march actually work?

Lori: Yes—I've seen such a structured process work—but there are key ingredients in this recipe that cannot be missing if all is to turn out well. First and foremost, a truly successful process depends on faculty leadership. At the same time the faculty's willingness to invest energy and political capital will very likely depend on the initial framing of the task. It would help if the financial dilemma is presented as an intellectually interesting puzzle rather than as a doomsday scenario. And, just as important is the provision of time and space for the task force to engage deeply in their learning and creative idea generation while also moving quickly through the process.

The success of such an endeavor depends on the quality of the human communication that occurs among task force members, between the task force and the administration, and in the campaign with the broader campus community. The disruption of COVID-19 is serving as a catalyst for acceleration of these types of task force discussions and decisions. If we can have this kind of money talk, the basic premise of this book will be realized: that we in higher education can communicate for a change, transforming higher education from the inside out.

The Students We Hardly Know

JOINING THE CONVERSATION: CHEYENNE CARRELL, Prescott College alum, and NEVAEH NEZ, University of Minnesota Rochester sophomore

Bob: Serving as a trustee is an exercise in feeling trapped between an unrepentant nostalgia and a nagging fear that the institution one serves is now at risk. That sweet-and-sour mix of troubled times and good memories is never more apparent than in the breaks between sessions when, as trustees, we gather to reminisce and reconsider. We tell stories of the time when we were on campus and of the professors and students who for us remain frozen in time. We share the indelible memories that we have gladly polished at every opportunity. And therein lies the problem. We recognize that we are in trouble; intellectually, we know today's students are different—their experiences are shaped by events that we too experience, but we face them as adults who have lived successful lives. Students are just beginning that journey and, as we would gladly remind them if they in fact were to ask, they have much to learn.

The problem that most trustees—along with the faculty who taught them—are only beginning to confront is that those same students are very different in a host of important ways—and age in years is only part of the equation. Today's students are in fact wired differently, with different fears and expectations that make them think differently than we did back then and do now. Just how different they are is highlighted in an important new book by Greg Lukianoff and Jonathan Haidt with the intriguing title *The Coddling of the American Mind*, which echoes Allan Bloom's 1987 best seller *The Closing of the American Mind: How Higher Education Has Failed Democracy and Impoverished the Souls of Today's Students*. Lukianoff and Haidt's initial focus was on freedom of speech issues that led them to ask why should this generation of college students, particularly those at elite institutions, aggressively seek to ban ideas they see as sexist, racist, and exclusionary. In the lingo of today, what these young people fight against are triggering behaviors. It is precisely the kind of behavior that the young are protected from and that Lukianoff and Haidt argue has produced the kind of protectionism that in time becomes coddling.

I first heard Haidt make this argument at a seminar at the Yale School of Management. What I remember most about his presentation, however, was his observation about changes in child rearing. He asked us if we—an audience of senior academics—remembered the first time we had been allowed to go to the corner store by ourselves. My answer was from about age six years old onward—I would simply hop on my bike and pedal the four blocks to the store, often in the company of a gang of like-minded ruffians. For today's young, Haidt observed, drawing on the kind of detailed behavioral data psychologists relish, the age of such independence is more likely to be twelve years or older. Until then, the young are protected. Haidt knows well that such coddling is uneven. If he is right, the students we teach in our colleges today are both free and coddled. They read and look at what they want on the Internet. They eat and imbibe whatever they can get their hands on. But at the same time they have lived part of their lives as adolescents protected by parents who have a strong sense of the kinds of behavioral freedoms that ought to be off limits—like walking to the corner store while still in elementary school.

Here is how Lukianoff and Haidt describe that most modern of a dilemmas, confessing oh so gently that

> we have always been ambivalent about the word "coddling." We didn't like
> the implication that children today are spoiled, pampered, and lazy, because

that is not accurate. Young people today—at a minimum, those who are competing for places at selective colleges—are under enormous pressure to perform academically and to build up a long list of extracurricular accomplishments. Meanwhile, all teens face new forms of harassment, insult, and social competition from social media. Their economic prospects are uncertain in an economy being reshaped by globalization, automation, and artificial intelligence, and characterized by wage stagnation for most workers. So most kids don't have easy, pampered childhoods. But as we will show in this book, *adults* are doing far more these days to protect children, and their overreach might be having some negative effects. Dictionary definitions of "coddle" emphasize this overprotection; for example, to "treat with extreme or excessive care or kindness." The fault lies with adults and institutional practices, hence our subtitle: "How Good Intentions and Bad Ideas Are Setting Up a Generation for Failure." That is exactly what this book is about. We will show how well-intentioned overprotection—from peanut bans in elementary schools through speech codes on college campuses—may end up doing more harm than good. (Lukianoff and Haidt 2018)

What follows from coddling and overprotection is what Lukianoff and Haidt call "safetyism," in which its adherents become frozen, perhaps even paralyzed, and unable to make "the reasonable trade-offs demanded by other practical and moral concerns." Less anyone missed the seriousness of this charge, Lukianoff and Haidt conclude, "Safetyism deprives young people of the experiences that their antifragile minds need, thereby making them more fragile, anxious, and prone to seeing themselves as victims" (Lukianoff and Haidt 2018).

My slightly less contentious conclusion is that our students really are different, much as the young in the 1960s were labeled as being both different and strange. Today's young are often remarkable problem solvers and gamers and at the same time much less likely to be readers. In imaginary worlds they are extraordinary explorers, but not so much in their daily lives except where the Internet is involved. In college they encounter curricula and faculty much more like us and markedly less like themselves. What they have to navigate almost from the get-go is a curriculum designed by us but not for them.

Last year, Susan Shaman, Susan Baldridge, and I published *The College Stress Test: Tracking Institutional Futures across a Crowded Market*. Much of that work simply reinforced what we and most followers of the market already knew. The market for an undergraduate education in the United States was one in which the rich institutions were getting richer and the big were getting bigger. As I noted earlier, the statistic that surprised and alarmed us, however, focused on the dropout rates among first-year students. More than half the four-year colleges and universities in the United States lost a quarter or more of their beginning students by the end of their first year—many of them by the end of their first semester. My suspicion is that the majority of those who dropped out encountered an educational experience that made little or no sense to them. What they wanted were jobs and a reasonably secure future, and what they found instead were diversions that in their minds led everywhere but where they wanted to go.

If I am right, then the monumental task facing our colleges and universities is a massive retooling of the undergraduate curriculum—a retooling that begins with and depends on a fundamentally different and more informed understanding of who our students are, what they want, and why.

Lori: Somehow, with two offspring in graduate school and a campus of undergraduates who are also precious to me, I feel immediately defensive on behalf of the students I think I know well but would like to know better. I'm glad you and the authors you quote place responsibility on parents and educational systems rather than suggesting something fundamentally negative about the young people themselves. And I agree that at the very least the curriculum needs to change if we are to adapt well to our students and our moment in history.

At this moment I am quarantined with my daughter, the second of my children I have sent on to graduate school. It's a momentary privilege I'm experiencing, to be able to listen and engage deeply with my daughter in person.

Our book's title—*Communicate for a Change*—isn't suggesting only that we "talk." Human communication necessarily involves both speaking and listening, so that mutual meaning-making can occur. If we are to know the students we seek to educate, we all have to keep listening—everyone who works in higher education needs an intentional, ongoing process that keeps us tuned in to our students. That means more than having a student sit on a committee, though such practices are vital. Remember Apaq's question? "What do you see when you look out?" We need to be able to answer that question, to attempt to listen deeply enough to see through the lens of the other. Listening like that requires that we accept the perspectives of "the other" (these students we need to know) as not right, not wrong—but absolutely real. To get started, read Reddit regularly or browse Rate My Professor.com. It takes a bit of bravery to listen to raw student commentary—but after all, we're not the snowflakes, right? Try the following exchange from Reddit: "So many young adults are knee deep in debt right now because they paid for an overpriced degree and now work at a job they could have gotten right out of high school," which drew this reply: "Absolutely not. I'm going to take a semester break if that happens [fall 2020 online education]. It's not worth my f*ing crazy tuition without labs, access to resources, and an environment to learn." Thirteen minutes later came the reply I really liked:

> I think there's just something very unnatural about communicating over Zoom. Ex: I was in a recitation of about 15 people that met once a week before break. The TA was awesome. She really pushed us to analyze the material and then share our thoughts with the class. Everyone constantly challenged each other in a healthy way. It was one of the few classes each week where we all wished it lasted longer. I learned a ton and really questioned a lot of my beliefs. After COVID, the TA set up the class on zoom with literally the exact same structure and it was AWFUL. A mix of awkward silences and people talking over each other. It was so difficult getting social cues on when you could interject. The discussions didn't feel like real conversations. She actually ended up canceling the recitation for the rest of the semester because everyone stopped logging on. (Reddit, May 7, 2020)

Importantly, most students reflect the same nostalgia you commented on at the opening of this chapter, though on Reddit it comes in a different form. From the same exchange on Reddit:

This semester is ending and it just feels like nothing. I usually get kind of sad when a semester ends. I think of the classes, the people, the routine and how much I've grown in those months . . . but this semester I feel nothing. My classes end this week, I have finals the following and I'm just like "can this boring ass crap be over already?" It 100% feels like a chore. I don't want to pay $5,000+ just to sit in my noisy ass house, watch some hastily slapped together lecture videos and do mindless busy work ever again. There is no experience. This is sh*t. (Reddit, May 8, 2020)

As we know, among the types of students least likely to graduate are those whose parents did not attend college. In an interview with *Inside Higher Ed* about her new book, *The Journey before Us: First-Generation Pathways from Middle School to College*, Laura Nichols describes the heart of the matter:

There is great work, such as that by Anthony Jack, about what elite colleges can do to welcome and graduate more low-income and first-generation students. These include addressing cultural biases as well as consistently reminding students that they belong at the school, are welcome there and are as qualified as students who come from college-going families. The first-generation students in my study pointed to a number of other issues across the range of postsecondary paths. Students needed help navigating complex degree requirements, financial aid and how to continue school when there were setbacks. Their experiences also showed that we must do more to bolster our public two- and four-year colleges if we are to grow the completion rates of first-generation students. (Nichols 2020b)

Here's the same perspective in student voice (again on Reddit):

Clueless First Generation College Freshman. Send Help. Hello everyone, I have a few questions and I know some of them may seem silly, but as the title suggests, I am a first generation college student trying to figure things out on my own and I have no clue who to ask, so here I am on Reddit! A bit of background information: I am a 21 year old freshmen. I do not qualify for FAFSA [free application for federal student aid] / federal loans for personal reasons, so my only option to pay for school is to take out private loans. Anyways, I was accepted to my state's university. When I found out I was accepted, I got really excited and couldn't wait for Fall, so I made a last minute decision to attend summer semester . . . which starts next week. I emailed my university asking if it was too late, and they informed me that (University) does not drop classes for non-payment and that instead I will get a $40 late fee and after 5 weeks I will start getting 1% interest and collection fees for every week that passes by. I can still attend my classes even if my payment does not come in time for the deadline. So, I know I messed up by not planning ahead and figuring stuff out. Again, I have no idea how any of this works and I'm completely on my own for this. My question is, when should I take out a loan and how much? Or should I just take out one loan for the entire four years I will be in University? So sorry for the silly questions and sorry for any grammar errors English is my second language! Any help would be appreciated, thank you so much. (Reddit, May 10, 2020)

Hundreds of comments followed.

Those who teach persuasion and public speaking describe the challenge of "knowing your audience" and "decentering your message." The structure of the argument, word choice, illustration types, and more all need to begin with the listeners' perspective, if the impact is designed to incite change—described in education as growth, development, or learning. So, yes Bob, let's radically revitalize the curriculum as well as the teaching and learning process, *after* we've listened well. We need to track the data and research about rates of anxiety and depression in young adults. We would benefit to read at least the summaries of neuroscience research on cognitive processing, learning, and trauma. We must build awareness of the impact of daily technology use on brain development and habits of mind. We ought also to engage in a scholarly deep dive on our students, moving well beyond glancing at Beloit's annual first-year student mindset list. There's a lot of evidence that needs our collective attention and respect. Big data disaggregated could be keenly informative, but the task of using what we learn about students to *adapt* is the part where we might still be stuck.

Student voices need to supplement those data. Genuine relationships with young people are paramount for all in higher education. True that for many professors, relationships with students provide meaning and even joy. Yet even for those who modify class discussions as they listen to student perspectives or who know some of their advisees quite well, systemic change rarely stems from that deeper personal connection. I often counseled communication majors as they chose between the requirements listed for the BA versus the BS. They were generally baffled when I attempted to explain the rationale for the "distribution" requirements (perhaps because I didn't quite get it myself). I worked to be clear and empathetic, thinking that was my only way to help. It didn't occur to me that I could change the curriculum beyond my department (at least, not for a while). So again, we're back to changes that take collective action by the faculty, and if we are ever to adapt, we will have to invest in conversations designed to revitalize the whole enterprise.

Bob: Lori, we are not so far apart, though again our different styles are readily apparent. Frankly, I would not push faculty to dive deeply into the neuroscience research on cognitive processing, learning, and trauma. It is an important literature, but one that is accessible only if one comes to it out of a sense of curiosity. We need to start by asking what we actually know about our students and that asking needs to take place largely in small groups with faculty colleagues. We need to promote the habit of listening to our students and then talking with them in settings as devoid of professorial authority as we can make them. But we also need to practice the art of talking about our students among ourselves—sharing openly and frankly the lessons we have learned in the classroom and elsewhere. I do believe it is those discussions that will spark the curiosity that is the necessary precursor to the kind of intellectual deep dive that you have called for.

Then the fun should begin. Using what we have learned from our conversations both with and about our students, we need to rethink our curricular processes by asking, "In addition to what students need to learn, how, when, and where should that learning take place?" I have no doubt that the collegiate curriculum emerging from such a process will be fundamentally different from what we offer our students today.

Lori: Yes! Fun indeed. And there are some good ideas out there already, like Georgetown University's "Designing the Future(s)" initiative, brain-child of its vice president for strategic education initiatives, Randall Bass. Students are brought together with faculty and staff for sustained conversation in a space reserved for that novel purpose—Georgetown's Red House:

> It's a space for innovation, a place to meet and share ideas, a place where faculty, staff, and students are coming together . . . in a "curriculum incuba-tor" to develop curricular experiments that break old boundaries and serve a new generation of students and alumni. Part design lab, part conference room, part coffee house, the Red House is a space uniquely dedicated to mapping new integrated curricular and co-curricular structures. . . . The Red House is where . . . transformative ideas become reality. (Georgetown University website)

These Red House conversations have generated new experiential learn-ing endeavors, including "core pathways" described for incoming stu-dents on Georgetown's website: "The Core Pathway allows you to fulfill core and elective requirements through an interdisciplinary collection of courses that address a complex global challenge. The focus of the first pathway is climate change. The second pathway which launched in the Fall of 2019 is on humanity and technology." Sustained conversation with students gave birth to these ideas, though faculty, staff, and administra-tors necessarily served as implementers. At Georgetown, and in other curricular reforms that honor student perspectives, the end results often build *relevance* and *curricular cohesion* by connecting students to purpose and potential impact. It's no surprise that engaged learning in creatively framed coursework can move students forward on essential learning out-comes. As students unpack the complexity and context of the problems they are driven to solve, the relevance of historical, sociological, eco-nomic, and other disciplinary lenses also becomes apparent.

What may need emphasis is that revitalized coursework and creative learning environments also connect readily to career exploration. As we engage in conversation with today's students, we hear again and again their deep worries about future employment. Let's circle back to a phrase that triggers many faculty: "preparing the future workforce." We can soften the linguistic blow by saying, "developing talent" to avoid the defense-raising inference that a college education is a "job training" program. Many of us are also justifiably sensitive to career-heavy language that may limit students' perceptions of the humanities as a viable option of study. Furthermore, we educators are nobly committed to preparing college-educated citizens to sustain and lead the democracy. Yes, *and* let's acknowledge that the students we hardly know are asking for a glimmering golden thread of connection between what they are learning in college and their first positions after college. Often, that thread is not obvious to students, as evidenced by their collective reaction to general education requirements. We can provide a remedy by speaking more explicitly to that concern, especially in early courses and with first-generation students. Integrated curriculum can (and does already, in many cases) accomplish the learning outcomes employers identify as most important. The 2018 Association of American Colleges and Universities employer survey results place oral communication, applying knowledge in real-world settings, and working effectively in teams at the top of the list. One way we need to adapt to our current students is to illuminate for them how what they are learning can be translated for future employers. Project-based, competency-generating, problem-focused coursework can make those potential connections crystal clear. Yet of course, that's not all students need us to know about them as we revitalize higher education.

While Kenneth Keniston may best be remembered among academics for founding MIT's innovative program in Science, Technology, and Society—designed to address "the most difficult and complicated problems facing humanity"—it is vital to note that he did so based on his enduring scholarly investigation of the social psychology of college students, beginning in the sixties. The desire of young people to make a difference, to connect and contribute, and our need to create relevant curriculum and engaged learning experiences may not be new. However, the context in which today's students enter into such work is new. Those who study the life-stage of emerging adulthood today include Satia Byock, a therapist and thought leader who focuses in part on what she identifies as the "quarter-life crisis." I talked to her on Mother's Day, 2020, as she hiked through the hills of her neighborhood in the Northwest on an unusually warm and dry afternoon, listening for insight with my daughter. Satia had a lot to say.

> Young adulthood is an extraordinarily generative period of life that out-
> lines the rest of our existence. . . . We need to listen to the "symptoms" of
> emerging adults as development and life-making, not diagnose them as a
> disorder. . . . Bipolar, anxiety—and other mental health diagnoses—all seem
> to onset when someone is in their twenties. . . . It's an incredibly challenging
> period of life. As they are struggling with their emotions in a world that
> seems like a disaster and with little foundation in how to take care of them-
> selves, young people who go to college encounter a kind of tortuous dictato-
> rial intellectualism that doesn't honor emotions or lived experiences. . . .
> Often their responses show up as neurotic, wounded, and uninformed when,
> culturally, young people are attempting to introduce emotion, personality,
> and individual experience into the learning. . . . We're missing something
> that is massively important. Students today are deeply emotional people,
> often coming out of family systems that are broken, not in genuine relation-
> ships. So, they feel anxious? Throw them on meds. The technology doesn't
> teach them how to be in relationship either. Click-bait isn't a real connec-
> tion. . . . And then, if their professor wants to play by old rules, saying that
> something is true or real because they say it is or because it's in a book,
> presenting facts as separated from experience, thinking their expertise is
> all the student needs—well, I'd suggest they go to therapy too. They are part
> of the system. . . . Intellectualism should not be a disembodied experience,
> absent of experience and emotion. One shouldn't have to learn about slavery
> without exploring what it felt like to be slave. . . . Everyone remembers the
> professors who were in their bodies as they talked, sharing themselves—and
> their experience with what they are teaching. You love those people; . . . they
> are not wasting your time. They are not wasting your money. They didn't get
> tenure a decade ago and are now phoning it in. They know what it feels like to
> feel. What makes anxiety go away? What enables young people to move from

childhood to adulthood? In the classroom and out, it's safety, healing, beauty—but most of all, it's relationship.

Bob: As you know I have been intrigued with what it is like to have a student back home, ready to reflect on what we have to say. I asked you to share with your daughter, Cheyenne, what we had written and see if she would be willing to write a response. Here's what she told us.

Cheyenne Carrell: Yes, we were coddled. But you need to take into account how we were socialized to have instant gratification and then sometimes we are being blamed for it. The consumerism culture of our childhoods was unbelievable. We were trained through social media marketing not to be able to sit with discomfort. That makes it tough to become educated.

Maybe the big contradiction of our generation—though you older people have your contradictions too—is that we young people can't tolerate the kind of change we're asking for. I think our generation's sensitivity is both a superpower and a curse. We see what's wrong and want it to be different—the climate, the corporate greed, the cost of higher education, the racist system, healthcare inequities—but we need to be more resilient to be able to make those changes happen. The government is not changing quickly enough, and the world isn't going to last very much longer.

If we're too sensitive in class, maybe faculty need to look in the mirror. I think they need to be taught how to facilitate class conversations among students with wildly varying points of view and cultural backgrounds. We live with so much political polarization. It would help if we had practice managing conflicts that rise from differences in relationships before we even got to college. It's hard, because we have been conditioned not to be able to deal with discomfort. But my experience shows that even some really great faculty lack the skill to facilitate those kinds of conflicts in the classroom.

After taking some awful classes at a campus I don't need to name here, I eventually went to Prescott College in Arizona. Most students, including me, were drawn there because we didn't fit into the mold of other colleges we had tried. Prescott's focus on sustainability and social justice connected us to purpose. But the problem now is that we don't really know how to translate our passion for people and the earth—and for living differently as a result of our awareness—into careers. Most of us figure out we need to go to grad school, and some of my college friends go back for something practical—like a nursing license—while trying to figure out how to live sustainably in a culture that makes that really difficult. And at the same time some of us have a lot of debt and no real way to pay it off. The principles I'm committed to keep me from wanting to cooperate with corporate greed. It's all overwhelming. Some of us want to live off the earth, build sustainable homes, but unless your family has money to support you, it's really hard. Don't get me wrong. I loved my professors and my college experience. We had a lot of choices about what we would study—which really worked for me. My first college experience was as bad as it gets—unqualified adjuncts and out-of-touch faculty, sometimes rambling off topic, sometimes sharing sexist opinions—giving us meaningless busy work assignments and multiple-choice exams—and a set of disconnected classes that were meeting some requirement categories that I never did understand. And then I just thought this is kind of worthless and not even interesting and it's costing money. And where is it leading? I don't want to get a job working in a corporation that helps the 1 percent and contributes to the destruction of the planet. I feel a lot of existential angst about how to live a sustainable life—eating local food, having a low carbon footprint without much money or hope about the future. And I'm not alone. That's part of the anxiety for us—we don't want to become perpetrators of the problems we want to change. I don't want to do that, but at the same time I have to exist within this system.

My voice is just one perspective, and one that comes with a certain level of privilege. We need to listen to many more young people, especially those who are systemically oppressed. The idea of "coddling" doesn't apply across the board.

Lori: For another perspective we turned to Nevaeh Nez, a first-generation college student, a sophomore studying health science at the University of Minnesota Rochester. Nevaeh is originally from the village of Hotevilla of the Hopi Tribe and now calls Flagstaff home (when she's not "up north" studying). She's aiming for both an MD and MPH, intending to return to her reservation to enhance healthcare accessibility for the Hopi people. A student leader on the campus I serve, Nevaeh joins our conversation:

Nevaeh Nez: So many Native American students like me don't even graduate from high school, so college isn't even an option. Our families want to protect us from being hurt by the outside world. They care about their little ones and want to make things simpler, not harder—if that's what you mean by coddling. Maybe the reservation seems easier, but there is a whole world out there you need to know, I think—and I challenge graduating Hopi students to go out of state, or leave the reservation, like I did. There is a lot to learn and it's worth it, even if it's hard.

My mom moved us off the reservation to a border town so we could be educated. The history of education is held back from students. Knowing the true history of education in this nation would help a lot in understanding why we are where we are. As a first-generation student, or Native American, or low income, or many other students from diverse backgrounds—the odds are stacked against you. There is so much extra work, besides the learning—like the FAFSA—that many first-generation students don't know how to manage so they can continue their education. In my high school, we created a commencement tradition of having Native American students wear tribal stoles at commencement to show respect for what we had accomplished. I carried that honor into my mindset about college. There aren't many Native American students here, but there are other first-gen students I can create that bond with. I've put my voice into leadership roles. Many minority students are hurt now by the history they don't even know, like what happened with public land grants in Minnesota.

In my culture, using your voice is sometimes not seen as being humble—they tell us not to brag. But I feel a responsibility to speak up. I saw my mom be lifted up by others investing in her, and in me—so I want to do the same. My sister showed me what was possible, getting her CNA [certified nursing assistant] while she was in high school—and her pre-health certificate from the community college—so I knew there was a path. And now,

I see that my young cousin and others on the reservation feel more capable and motivated if they know what is possible. And for that to happen, I need to use my education as a platform, to be visible to other native youth. My tribe is concerned about their youth for many reasons—so there is some bumping of heads, though it's changing through discussions with elders. Actually, being away makes me more interested in knowing the ceremonies and not forgetting my culture, and eventually I will also have something to offer back to my community.

I wonder what can create a movement to transform higher education, and I think it's about students getting into relationships with faculty and making connections with everyone we can. I tell other students, it might seem scary because they have education and you don't yet, but if we can find things we both care about, then we can collaborate to ensure all kinds of students are getting what was promised by the education system. I tell my fellow students that we have so much power within us that we just need to use. The power is in voice and it's worth using it. People will listen to diverse and unique students because your voice is different. You would think that uniqueness is what would hold you back, but it's really what will take you forward, if you use your voice to connect, to apply for special programs, and to talk with faculty and other people who don't know your perspective.

The faculty need to be willing to connect when students reach out, though. I have some great professors, but I would ask all professors and college leaders to be more open about what is going on in today's society—showing they're open for discussion of all kinds of topics, you know—open to having real conversations with students. And that means listening to students and asking them questions, and also being active outside of the classroom and more public about that activism. If they are interested in listening to my perspective, I would ask them to open their minds and become educated on topics outside of their specialty. They might want to start with the histories of education they probably don't even know, and how those histories have affected their students.

Lori: Both Neveah and Cheyenne are in the circle of students I know and care about. Some might say, "hey—that's a sample of convenience"—your home campus and your home. I agree, but instead of apologizing, I urge you to do the same. Start a conversation with the closest college students you can find. Ask questions and listen to the answers. *Why are you in college? How did you decide to continue your education? What do you find challenging? Some say young people have been coddled, overprotected—and that all that help in childhood doesn't prepare you well for college. What is your experience? Why do you think college costs what it does? Describe your most vibrant online learning experience. If you were designing a new college, what is the first change you would make?* These first conversations may inform additional questions you can continue to ask students from a wide array of perspectives, but what is imperative is that you and the other change-makers on your campus talk to each other about what you learn from these students whom we need to know. We challenge you to launch an ongoing forum in which faculty and other higher education professionals (including administrators) listen to student and young alumni voices and then talk with each other about what they've heard, sharing themes broadly in department meetings, curriculum committees, budget hearings, board meetings, and more. As together we reimagine higher education post-COVID-19, let's start the redesign with the learners and their learning in mind.

Is It Ever Safe to Talk about Changing the Curriculum?

JOINING THE CONVERSATION: MARK PUTNAM, president, Central College

Bob: Among the other things I have learned from our rumbles is that there are two quite different kinds of conversations higher education has been avoiding. The most disruptive are those that involve entrenched taboos—subjects that are truly dangerous to talk about. Discussions of race and gender involve such taboos, as do extended conversations about money or about governance or even about the mess we are in. The other kind of conversations we avoid are those that are just too difficult as well as exhausting or just plain unpleasant. Topping my list of such conversations are aborted attempts to spur curriculum reform. I have long puzzled about why curricular reform is such a deadly non-topic across American higher education. It was also the topic Greg Wegner, Ann Duffield, and I explored in *Making Sense of the College Curriculum*. You, Lori, were part of this adventure as well when you became one of the ten collectors of faculty stories that made the book possible. In *Making Sense* we came to argue that the challenge facing any attempt to change an undergraduate curriculum was best understood as a kind of Frostian riddle involving a choice between two important, but as it turned out, two opposing goals.

Here's how we put it in *Making Sense*: "Why . . . has there been so little curricular change? . . . Why do student transcripts resemble menu cards for the kind of learning smorgasbords that *Integrity in the College Curriculum* inveighed against so vehemently? Why is the three-credit course and the four-year degree still the standard almost everywhere? Why have assessment and accreditation proved to be such weak prods in the struggle to make an undergraduate education more affordable?" (Zemsky, Wegner, and Duffield 2018).

On the other hand, the pursuit of *pedagogical* change became the challenge championed by a host of successful organizations committed to improving teaching and learning. These efforts took advantage of the fact that pedagogical change was largely an individual response to the altered circumstances faculty were encountering everywhere.

> It was the kind of change that did not challenge the faculty member's personal control of what was taught, when, where, or how. Change remained individualistic—a matter of what I do in my classroom. One seldom, if ever, needed to ask permission of someone else in order to change how one taught. Pedagogical change not only left intact, but actually reinforced, the individual faculty member's sense of personal space and independence, of self and personal success. (Zemsky, Wegner, and Duffield, 2018)

What *Making Sense of the College Curriculum* documented was that sometime in the past 30 years there really was a moment when higher education chose, though never quite consciously, the other road, the one easier to travel, always promising itself that it could come back later to the challenge of curricular reform, though it never did. While it is the first stanza of Robert Frost's "The Road Not Taken" (1916) that is most often recalled, from our volume's perspective, it is the third stanza that contains the kernel of truth we were pursuing:

> And both that morning equally lay
> In leaves no step had trodden black.
> Oh, I kept the first for another day!
> Yet knowing how way leads on to way,
> I doubted if I should ever come back.

What our story-collecting taught us is simple to summarize. Curricular change, unlike pedagogical innovation, requires collective action. A whole system has to be changed, often in its entirety. Everyone must adapt to the new rules, including all those folks not at all certain that change is either necessary or desirable. Earlier we talked about the "missing we" in higher education, particularly among the faculty. It is a truism that particularly applies to curricular reform. One final observation. What we miss most is a cadre of heroes—faculty with political moxie who believe that only through curricular reform can higher education address what ails us. But doing so will take extraordinary energy and more than a little luck.

Lori: Energy. Luck. Or maybe, just maybe—a crisis: what you have called elsewhere, a "dislodging event." With COVID-19, we're certainly there—dislodged, disrupted, distressed. Bob, earlier you shared that your publisher didn't want to use "Is It Closing Time?" as the title of your most recent book, because no college president would want to be seen carrying that volume across campus. Right now, presidents aren't able to stroll their campuses, but many are asking that question as they speculate about the future from the isolation of their home offices and in the Zoom rooms they share with colleagues. I've engaged in such conversations, and I'm hearing about them from other campus leaders across the county. In one setting, a president has charged a task force to examine options to reduce costs in academics and research, while sustaining the mission. From all accounts, it's the kind of problem-solving group you and I are recommending for this set of conversations on the intractable issues that keep us idling instead of moving forward. Here's what that group may well need to succeed: a charge from the president; a specific assignment with a short timeline; members who are respected campus citizens; and, not least, a skilled facilitator presiding over the group's meetings. I have been part of such a group. In our first meeting we processed our charge and organized our work. We started with a reference to a potential effort to find course duplicates across colleges, using the example of "Intro to Statistics." What followed was quite a long pause. Then came a firm caution from a senior member: "You can't touch courses, because then you're touching the curriculum. You can't touch the curriculum, because then you're touching faculty numbers. And, you can't, you know, you absolutely cannot ever go there, or there'll be mutiny." And what does a mutiny look like? Perhaps unionization, for campuses where that's not already the reality. Perhaps faculty "no confidence" votes for the president? At the least, a demoralizing poke at the festering perception that there's a plot brewing to question the privileges tenured faculty have earned. And who wants to begin a descent down that slippery slope? No one, apparently, unless the governing board declares "financial exigency" and assumes enhanced decision-making authority.

But friends, where else shall we look to save money in an enterprise that had become difficult for students to afford, even before the current crisis? We can't tear down buildings, or stop servicing their debt. Administrator salaries are being slashed all over the country, as we speak—though many would argue there is more room for savings there. And still, still?—we are afraid to touch the curriculum for fear that all will topple? Shall we lop off research institutes, programs, and even campuses, to avoid a strategic, honest, holistic gaze at the curriculum? To do such work well would take interdisciplinary, cross-college, and in university systems—multicampus faculty teams. Employers might need to be consulted. Research-based practice could be a guiding light. Bottom lines would need clarity.

I know that faculty can do this kind of courageous, principled work together. I have been a witness. You like to say that I'm a testifier, and perhaps you are right. At the University of Wisconsin Oshkosh, a regional comprehensive university, we faced a crisis that didn't feel like a crisis to faculty but most certainly mattered to administrators worried about accreditation. The general education curriculum had languished for decades without a collective update, and reform attempts had been met with organized resistance. As one of the leaders of the eventually successful reform, I need to clear my conscience and admit that early on I was part of the resistance. In the late nineties, my chair shared with the department that "some group" had "gone behind closed doors" and without consultation from any of us determined that the introductory communication course would no longer be required. Apparently, she mentioned toward the end of her lengthy chair's report, this course reduction was a component of some sort of sweeping attempt to change general education. We faculty were appalled, as were the many instructors who taught multiple sections of that course as their sole teaching load. Their jobs were at risk. And then there was the *principle* of the thing! Who were these people and who gave them the authority to decide that communication, central to all of human experience and vital in every career, was no longer important enough to warrant even one measly 3-credit course in a 120-credit degree? We showed up at the open forum en masse to protest this pending abomination and to protect the required course that validated our place in the liberal arts.

Yup. That was me. Later, when I was the person facilitating data-driven conversations to revitalize general education, I often held space (and my tongue). I knew that proposed changes to course requirements could signal that someone was questioning the inherent value of the discipline to which others had devoted their life's work. From the outside, it might look like a protection of power, but the resistance was more than ego-defense, to be sure. It was partly about identity, partly about disciplinary dignity, partly about recruiting majors, and partly about some of those "words that ensnare"—like *academic freedom* and *faculty governance*. And at that point in the institution's history, over 800 courses comprised the menu from which 18-year-olds could choose to meet requirement categories. How to get from the extreme of course-by-course justification to a holistic analysis of student learning over time? Data were key, along with student voice. The data showed vast gaps in degree completion, with specific general education courses as the consistent impediment for underrepresented students. And we couldn't look away when surveyed students deemed general education courses "worthless."

At one point, someone from the College of Nursing asked, "Could you say that anyone who passes Comm 111 with a C or better is a competent communicator?" I knew that would be bogus. Ultimately, we investigated learning outcomes, only to discover that the course diminished communication apprehension (a noble result) but did not produce public speaking competence (by our own measure of the construct). Now what? It didn't take long to imagine how communication competence could be taught, with embedded assignments across the four-year curriculum. But that would take cooperation and people teaching outside their area of expertise. With a quick check we found that senior-level capstone courses in other disciplines were ignoring the scholarship on public speaking and giving silly advice, like "imagine them in their underwear" or "look above their heads."

And now, Bob, we diverge. I am convinced that the two paths of pedagogical innovation and curriculum reform need to intertwine if revitalization is to occur, even in the current crisis. While enhancing one's teaching *can* be done as a solo sport, that has not been characteristic of the scholarship of teaching and learning movement or many other faculty development endeavors. Data that demonstrate how simulations or flipped instruction enhance learning outcomes are not discipline-specific. For example, the high-impact practices discerned through a comprehensive literature review by the Association of American Colleges and Universities require cooperation across the curriculum in addition to adaptation of teaching within courses—community engagement, learning communities, common intellectual experiences, undergraduate research, collaborative learning, and more. In the case of my first campus, the momentum produced by teaching-focused faculty development led to broad awareness of the need for cooperative curricular reform. On my current innovation-focused campus, student learning data are used routinely for pedagogical and curricular decisions. Recently, an interdisciplinary team looked at the data and decided, together, that math would be taught just in time to be used in chemistry, with an unusual sequence and flipped instruction. Once faculty, especially those who teach undergraduates, can look at their courses as part of a whole (not my course but rather our curriculum), one more vital connection occurs. In her extraordinary poetic voice, Kate Light writes (2003):

There comes the strangest moment in your life,
When everything you thought before breaks free—
what you relied upon, as ground-rule and as rite
Looks upside down from how it used to be.

. . . .

How many people thought you'd never change?
But here you have. It's beautiful. It's strange.

Bob: I am not sure *diverge* is the right word—*collide* might be more descriptive of our differences in terms of defining the role curricular change needs to play in the reshaping of the undergraduate experience. You want to fix the curriculum while simultaneously accelerating the recasting of teaching practices and expectations. Frankly I want more. I want to abandon that dominant set of collegiate curricula whose principal rationale has been to promote disciplinary truth and departmental consensus.

The factoid that troubles me most is the observation that at more than half of the nation's colleges and universities a quarter or more of the institution's first-year students will be gone by next fall. Even institutions with "good" first-year student retention numbers generally can count on only about 80 percent of their first-year students returning for their sophomore year. The explanations for such slippage are many: those who dropped out weren't college ready; or they never developed the necessary sense of belonging; or they ran out of money; or even that they didn't want to go to college in the first place. Potentially valid explanations all. I am simply not convinced. Could it not be that the best explanation is that the first-year curricula most American undergraduates encounter is seen, as the surveyed students at your former institution so inelegantly put it, "a waste of my time and my money"? I know I am calling back to our previous conversation, which focuses on the students we no longer know. But I want to say here as well as there, that my case for radically revitalizing undergraduate education in the US begins with the claim that what is needed is a fundamentally different curriculum—one that is shorter, three years and 90 credits rather than four years and 120 credits; that begins with skills rather than general education sequences largely designed to introduce beginning students to disciplinary majors; and that unabash-edly takes advantage of what today's students do best: play complex games and solve puzzles.

Lori, I often use your institution as an example of what's possible. Your predecessor as chancellor, Steve Lehmkuhle, wanted a truly problem-solving curriculum. One of the innovations he and the faculty agreed to was substituting a year-long course in statistics for the standard first-year calculus sequence. What that experiment uncovered was that statis-tics made more sense for their pre-health and pre-med majors than did calculus—fewer confused and disoriented learners, more successful first-year students, many of whom went on in their second year to succeed in a calculus sequence. Statistics simply made more sense to UMR's begin-ning students who were strong problem solvers—they flourished when called upon to use their gaming and related skills. Steve had the advantage of a very small math faculty in an interdisciplinary department that wasn't in-clined to fight this perceived marginalizing of mathematics as a discipline.

Most faculty, particularly those with appointments in one of the classic liberal arts departments, are much more prepared for a fight to the death. Their curricula are all about securing enough majors to keep their depart-ments viable. There is seldom conversation about how one department's curriculum meshes with another. There is, for all intents and purposes, no design to their curriculums, just lists of requirements and choices, as in two from column A and two more from columns B and C. It is a circum-stance that works for almost all faculty and those students who fit the standard mold of a college learner. Students who want something else are simply out of luck. The result is that we continue curricular traditions that yield unacceptable first-year dropout rates.

In our conversation about why so many outside of higher education have come to see faculty members like us as "the bad guys," we laid out a program of curricular reform that began with a fulsome admission that what we have now is not working. There I also argued that everything ought to be on the table—no sacred cows left unperturbed. What we need to get started is a full, frank, and public acknowledgment of past mistakes and misunderstandings. Such an acknowledgment becomes the sine qua non that promises survival. The question at hand—I know I have taken an embarrassingly long time to get to this moment of truth—is, how do we talk ourselves into making the requisite changes that we have come at last to acknowledge must be made? What would such a conversation sound and look like?

Lori: To start the conversation constructively, an interdisciplinary team would benefit from a fresh slate and a campuswide set of reform principles, determined by consensus—as well as the space to think *way out of the box*. Those principles would necessarily include an intense *focus on students and their learning*, with an absolute commitment to begin with a deep dive into the *data* (both qualitative and quantitative, campus-specific as well as state and national). I'm aware of at least one Office of Institutional Research unwilling to share DFW rates by course for fear of offending a department or embarrassing a faculty member (this at an institution with research as part of its core mission). So, yeah, that mandatory commitment to stare at reality will take courage. While relevant data may be found in IR offices, other data need to see campuswide (or systemwide) daylight as well—such as how learning is being measured, how course grades are determined, what employers identify as core competencies, how much instruction costs and what drives those expenditures, and much more. In some cases, robust documentation of students' progress toward learning outcomes has not occurred (especially if faculty have resisted or dismissed all things "assessment"). On those campuses, the basic backwards design process will be a starting point as together they ask, "What should a graduate of our campus know and be able to do?" and then—"How will we know that such learning has transpired?"—and ultimately, "How can we work together to construct interlocking, intentional learning experiences to accomplish those aims?"

The "clean slate" commitment can be an innovation accelerator. At Oshkosh, there was a privileged moment in time that allowed the dean of the College of Letters and Science to pledge that no faculty lines would be lost to the curricular reform. Given that context, some fear and defensiveness subsided and *eventually* faculty agreed to a guiding set of principles—

and (miraculously) they also agreed that on a given day all 800+ gen ed courses would be eliminated. To opt into the new program, faculty could participate in coordinated course creation seminars (small stipend provided). Most reported the experience was intellectually stimulating and enriching. One rather stoic, longtime associate dean returned to teaching full time, regularly and gleefully reporting personal reinvigoration at a late stage in his career. Much of that invigoration came from the positive student response to the new courses and teaching approaches, while some of it was generated from the enjoyment and novelty of disciplinary collisions that occurred in the professional development experience.

We are asking, "Is it ever safe to talk about changing the curriculum?" Knowing that many attempts at curricular reform have failed across all types of campuses, I'm also thinking about what successful curricular revitalization conversations do *not* sound and look like. So, how do participants derail these conversations?

- Debating the value of one discipline over another. Everyone is sure to lose when core value is attacked.
- Citing current curricular procedures or policies that automatically make such-and-such an idea impossible or overly time-consuming. Those can be changed!
- Repeating past stories of administrative overstep or failed attempts to coordinate curriculum across departments or colleges, diminishing trust in colleagues and leaders. At some point, these recollections need to go in a "parking lot" so that we can say, "From now on" instead of "up until now" or "watch out" or "that'll never work because."
- Referencing the "accreditors" as a menacing overlord, lurking nearby and sure to threaten any attempt at curricular innovation. We need to know the guardrails, but new curricula with a clear student learning focus and a commitment to evidence-based decisions are unlikely to lead to accreditation challenges.
- Dismissing current student learning data or spending inordinate amounts of conversation time searching for explanations to

invalidate results—to avoid talking about the problem that has been illuminated.

- Reminding participants that there is no money available to support innovation. That claim assumes the curricular innovation will be added on to what already exists. Instead, these conversationalists have the opportunity to create and design new approaches to higher education that are also cost-effective (provided they have also had the Money Talk).
- Pointing to a specific faculty member or department as a known blockade to new ideas, as though every dissenter has veto power (or that minds cannot be changed).
- Excluding constituents or avoiding consultation with groups assumed to be hostile. Neglecting to share emerging ideas broadly with the campus community throughout the process can create blind spots or derail implementation.
- Separating teaching and learning practice from curricular reform. (For example, if we're moving to competency-based learning and block scheduling simultaneously, imagine the potential for a truly elegant design that elevates teaching and learning, enhances students' sense of belonging, and simultaneously streamlines the curriculum.)
- Ignoring valid, reliable, relevant research.

While these common conversation killers can be called out, knowing what to avoid may ultimately be less valuable than knowing how to begin. To stimulate the collective imagination, perhaps we need to launch these campus conversations with one clear question: *"What would we do with the curriculum if we were starting from scratch?"*

Bob: It's the right question, but I fear it will at best lead to marginal changes in college curricula that will evaporate over time. Unless I am simply misunderstanding your argument, you are seeking accelerated business as usual. You don't really imagine changed processes—but I do. I introduced Wallace's notion of a revitalization movement because it is a process of fundamental change—perhaps the only way open to us. It is a process that begins with a full and frank acknowledgment that what we have been doing is wrong—not just inadequate but truly and wondrously wrong.

Changing the curriculum I have now argued requires a fundamentally different kind of conversation. Here what is required is literally an erasing of presumptions about learning that have held sway since at least the Second World War. And the requisite conversation will no doubt challenge, as no other major reform does, the primacy of the faculty. The latter is an admission that there is hope for success only if those with the most to lose actually lead the process. What is required is an unfettered revival that allows faculty to imagine a truly different curricular future.

Conversations both about differences and about the curriculum are essential. But up until now neither has been infused with sufficient energy to make the necessary changes happen. And here is perhaps the final irony. Were each of these conversations to be convened simultaneously, the one focusing on the curriculum might well conclude with a non-emotional recasting of the processes by which institutions determine their curricula. At the same time, the conversation focusing on difference might well conclude with what might best be called a passionate reaffirmation of the importance of equity and inclusion.

Mark Putnam is an old friend who for nearly a dozen years has been president of Central College in Iowa. He joins the conversation.

Mark Putnam: Permit me to reframe the conversation just a bit. You both make important points about the conditions needed to advance a comprehensive conversation regarding curricular change. My task is now to take you back to the beginning of this conversation and test the remedies you are describing against the presenting conditions.

In the late 1980s, I enrolled in my first graduate class at Teachers College, Columbia University. The course was titled "Organization and Administration of Higher Education," taught by Robert Birnbaum. His book *How Colleges Work* was completed but had not yet been released. Accordingly, we were given copies of the manuscript as our principal text for the semester.

Early in the course Birnbaum organized a simulation exercise. At the beginning of the session we were randomly assigned to one of four categories: student, administrator, trustee, or faculty member. We were then given very little information, but we knew we were affiliated with a research university. After a bit of organizing, the group of students reentered the room protesting a hot topic in those years, "Star Wars" research, more formally referred to as the Strategic Defense Initiative. Essentially, this was a Reagan-era effort to employ a space-based defense system to counter the Soviet nuclear threat. University-based defense research was quite controversial at that time. The student protesters delivered to us a pamphlet outlining students' concerns and demands. We were then sent immediately to separate rooms with no further instruction.

The exercise was fascinating in that each constituent group without prompting took on the stereotypical role—with trustees demanding answers, faculty demanding academic freedom, and administrators running between rooms to negotiate a path forward. A critic of this simulation might argue that we were simply role-playing. However, what became obvious is that we had been socialized into our assumptions regarding these roles and those social constructs proved to be quite reliable. That experience has stayed with me through the years and has been reinforced as I have interacted daily with each of these constituent groups.

Most relevant to this conversation is the simple fact that faculty members are socialized into a collective, dare I say, tribal framework of understanding. Repeatedly throughout my career I have had private conversations with faculty members who made statements to me such as, "I really believe we need to make a significant change to (fill in the blank), but I will never vote for it because I will never vote against my colleagues."

The macroscale challenge is informed by other concepts articulated by Birnbaum, including the high level of inertia associated with institutions of higher education, the lack of rationality in decision making, and the dynamics of organization best described as loosely coupled systems. The result of all this is an organization that is inherently resistant to change.

Every example I know of real systemic change in higher education at the national scale has grown from evolving externalities or abrupt crises.

The Industrial Revolution, the Morrill Land Grant Acts, world wars, the GI Bill, Sputnik, *Brown v. Board of Education*, and information technology are all examples of evolutionary pathways or crises that have ushered in periods of wide-ranging curricular change.

Absent these macro-level impacts, the change of a curriculum at the micro level tends to come at a glacial pace in the framework of collective action. On occasion it is born of an institutional crisis in which administrative authority is the animating force, typically owing to financial realities. Every once in a while, however, on a single campus the stars align; conversation leads to a shared vocabulary and an emerging narrative. Gradually that process results in guiding principles and a more or less shared curricular vision. The conditions for change are then present as conversation eventually leads to collective action. Informal faculty leadership seems to be a key ingredient. On my own campus, comprehensive curricular commitments over the past few decades to promote international education, sustainability, and writing across the curriculum were all born of faculty conversations later followed by collective action.

Your notions regarding the power of conversation are quite compelling but are also highly contextual. Conversation is rooted in communal experience and in my view can only be nurtured when a sufficient level of trust within a faculty is present. Initiating a conversation regarding curricular reform is really a family meeting in the setting of a household. It assumes a level of relational authenticity, not free of conflict, but one in which a sense of collective will is greater than the combined macro force of institutional inertia and the micro force of individual interest. That kind of shared commitment can produce substantive and meaningful curricular change.

Lori: Mark brings us back again to the trust prerequisite. What encourages me about having these challenging campus conversations is that the conversation itself has the potential to generate the necessary trust. Rather than being an excuse for not proceeding with curricular revolution, a lack of trust can be remedied by sustained and inclusive interaction. While this eighth conversation already includes many specific recommendations for getting started, here is one more: For all who will be asked to participate in campus "money talks" in response to the financial fallout from COVID-19—please insist that *revitalizing the curriculum* is on the short list of priorities to address with creativity and courage.

· conversation 9

Why Can't We Have a Productive Conversation about Race and Gender?

JOINING THE CONVERSATION: FREEMAN A. HRABOWSKI, president, University of Maryland Baltimore County (UMBC); PETER H. HENDERSON, senior advisor, Office of the President, and policy fellow, School of Public Policy, UMBC; and J. KATHLEEN TRACY, associate professor, School of Medicine, University of Maryland, and ACE Fellow at UMBC

Lori: New Harmony, Indiana, sits on its riverbank in living tribute to an unusual past. In 1824, secularist Robert Owen and others traveled down the Wabash River in a craft they called the *Boatload of Knowledge*. Having purchased the town from religious utopians who had tired of their celibate wait for the second coming, Owen and his colleagues aimed to create a different kind of utopia, which they called a Community of Equality—to be produced by education for all. They denounced slavery and supported equal rights for women. While the town's ideals and impact serve as a case study worth investigating (and it's still a fascinating place to visit), the imagined outcomes of the utopian community have not materialized— not in Indiana nor any other state. Campus by campus, region by region, we in higher education have failed to create communities of equality, despite our boatload of knowledge.

Let's start with some truth-telling. In the United States and its academies, the history of slavery, the colonization of native peoples, and the oppression of many others, including women, has not yet been reckoned with in ways that produce equity. Conversations that could move us forward are few, and the examples of continued affronts like the Silent Sam statue on the campus of the University of North Carolina are many. While there are many scholars like Ibram Kendi, Beverly Daniel Tatum, and Robin DiAngelo who bring expertise to these topics, Bob, you and I do not. We read. We listen. We seek to be active allies, practicing the principles of civil discourse. We advocate for programs to increase access and attainment—and to embolden the work of restorative justice. And at the same time, we are keenly aware that we lack credibility because our perspectives are informed by privilege—the visible and invisible advantages provided to us as white people in the United States. Bob, you have the added privilege of being male. We both lack scholarly expertise on these subjects, yet we are still both citizens and higher education professionals who need to talk purposefully about the history of differences and a path forward that yields transformed policies and practices.

One more truth. We've been cautioned not to even have this conversation. But here we go—and we're asking you to go with us. In his book *How to Be an Antiracist* Ibram Kendi asks us to inspect our definitions carefully: "With the word itself becoming radioactive to some, passé to others, some well-meaning Americans started consciously and perhaps unconsciously looking for other terms to identify racism. 'Microaggression' became part of a whole vocabulary of old and new words—like 'cultural wars' and 'stereotype' and 'implicit bias' and 'economic anxiety' and 'tribalism'—that made it easier to talk about or around the R-word" (Kendi 2019).

Before the tragic events of May 2020, my state was known for being "Minnesota nice." What many people knew about my adopted state was captured in Garrison Keillor's description of Lake Wobegon as the place "where all the women are strong, all the men are good-looking, and all the children are above average." Much more is now known about Minnesota. When its educational outcomes are disaggregated by race and focused on completion of high school and college, we are near the bottom of the list of states—a list leaving us little to brag about when it comes to equity. Before last spring's outpouring of grief and anger, important conversations had begun about how to change things.

One of those speaking out was Lt. Governor Peggy Flanagan, a member of the White Earth Ojibwe and the highest-ranking Native American to hold elected office in the United States. In her January 10, 2019, inaugural speech, she talked about the impact of policy on her childhood. "I was that kid with the different colored lunch ticket. We needed those free meals at school. . . . Medicaid saved my life. As a kid with asthma it's the reason I'm alive today." She went on to acknowledge racist policies from earlier eras of the office she now serves: "An office that oversaw horrific treatment of my ancestors. An office whose governor once declared that our Dakota brothers and sisters, and I quote, 'Must be exterminated or driven forever beyond the borders of Minnesota.'" She then expressed gratitude for the previous administration's repudiation of that racist language in a governor's eighteen-sixties declaration and added, "Our future is bright. 'One Minnesota' [the new administration's framing phrase for its policies] is grounded in the fact people directly affected by the decisions have a seat at the table" (Flanagan 2019). And her colleague, Governor Tim Walz, used the inauguration platform to reinforce the current need and priority: "We must dedicate ourselves now [to] make Minnesota the education state for all children—black, white, brown, indigenous" (Walz 2019).

Lt. Governor Flanagan and Governor Walz call our collective attention to three essential elements that need to inform conversations about racism and education, if they are to be constructive and effective: history, policy, and practice. Says Kendi, "Americans have long been trained to see the deficiencies of people rather than policy. It's a pretty easy mistake to make: People are in our faces. Policies are distant. We are particularly poor at seeing the policies lurking behind the struggles of people" (Kendi 2019). With leadership committed to educational transformation in this nice northern state, will new policies informed by history change practice? At this writing, everything is speculative. Before the murder of George Floyd in Minneapolis, the legislative session had opened and a constitutional amendment was being proposed by unlikely allies Neel Kashkari, president of the Federal Reserve Bank of Minneapolis, and Alan Page, a former Minnesota Viking and state Supreme Court justice. The amendment was framed as a mechanism to ensure equity in educational outcomes, though the state teachers' union is not in support. Governor Walz told the *Minneapolis Star Tribune*, "We're willing to explore it, because what we have been doing has not been working," adding that the proposed amendment is "a great conversation starter" (Van Oot 2020). Many are weighing in, from nonprofits to the state's chambers of commerce. Among them is Michael Ciresi, a former Democratic candidate for the US Senate and well-known trial attorney who leads a nonprofit organization, Our Children MN. Says Ciresi, "The citizens of Minnesota would like to have an honest, candid, frank discussion about this and that's what this amendment on the ballot will do" (Van Oot 2020). Kashkari adds, "The idea is not to be having the same conversations 20 years from now" (Van Oot 2020).

Are these broad constituency groups prepared to have these conversations, spanning policymakers, parents, and practitioners at all levels, including the multitude of voices of those who have been historically excluded? Higher education is not only a collective of practitioners who need to enact antiracist pedagogical, curricular, governance, and other changes; many scholars within our collective have vital research results to add to such conversations. Our participation in the broader dialogue depends in part on progress related to previous topics in this book: *Can we expand our identities to include a self-description as "educators," enabling us to link arms across disciplines and with those who teach our students before we meet them? In so doing, do we have the will to create a sustaining community that both nourishes and catalyzes us? Can we together assert the distinct value our perspective provides while also respecting the perspectives of those whom our enterprise has previously excluded? Can we—with our many types of expertise—humbly but effectively serve as facilitators of civil discourse on this topic, convening diverse stakeholders, reflecting on historical and current evidence with vulnerable authenticity, moving to action, measuring results, and adapting to the evidence with agility?* What a rumble that would be.

Bob: Lori you speak truth, but I fear you have opened this conversation in a way that will likely distract us. In our present context, conversations about differences that open with an apology and an offer of cultural reparation are more likely to exacerbate than soothe, satisfying some but not all. They may well offer an outlet for the emotions engendered by a focus on race and gender, but enough is never enough—or from the outset too much. What I think we seek instead are conversations that are problem solving, that tamp down emotions rather than inflame them, and that, when successful, offer the community a purposeful way forward.

I understand well that my observations will not be welcome by those who think the only way forward is a conversation that forces a frank reckoning by all those who benefit, mostly silently, from positions of privilege. I learned this lesson again just last week when I addressed a board of trustees worried about the future their institution faced. I began by presenting the institution's market position and reporting its market stress score. There followed a presentation inspired by our work on the conversations higher education needs to have but almost always avoids. Last on my list of too-long-avoided conversations was the one we're having now focusing on race and gender. Sitting with the trustees were three newly appointed African American senior officers, and they were visibly unhappy. What they lamented most was my call for conversations that purposefully tamped down emotions, which one of them labeled as "white conversations" as opposed to the kind of free-ranging conversations he wanted. And then the nickel dropped. What he was concerned with was who owned the conversation, who was in charge, who was in control. A "white conversation" in his mind would perpetuate the injustices of the past.

It was an exchange that made me see differently what you and I need to be about. The first conversations we proposed, for example, "Why Can't We Talk about the Mess We're In?" (conversation 1) or the "The Slogans That Ensnare Us" (conversation 3) were to be open-ended gatherings, quite literally the more the better. I now understand better that a campus conversation about differences would need to be more like our proposed conversation about money–that is, it would need to be problem focused, involving initially a small group of campus-citizens who had accepted the challenge of developing specific proposals within a given period of time. It is equally important who convenes that conversation. I think if we are talking about a university or a college, then the president needs to be the convener. There needs as well to be an agreed-upon starting point and initial set of problems to address, and that too is the responsibility of the president. To be sure, the agenda could change as the group worked through the problems it was charged with addressing—but it should not lose sight of the fact that it was specially charged with recommending specific actions to address specific challenges like how to increase the proportion of students of color or faculty of color or to implement curricular programs that focus on the experiences of people of color.

I have an example of what I think can work, drawn from efforts to confront gender discrimination in the sciences. In the late 1990s, Nancy Hopkins, a senior professor and molecular biologist at the Massachusetts Institute of Technology began agitating for a more even-handed distribution of opportunities for the institute's women faculty—better labs, more funded graduate students and postdocs, and greater recognition of their achievements by the institute. Her mini-campaign struck a nerve, leading MIT's President Charles Vest to appoint a committee chaired by Professor Hopkins herself to explore the distribution of opportunities and privileges across the institute. Vest, in conveying the committee's report to the MIT faculty, testified to what he had personally learned from Hopkins and her colleagues:

> I commend this study of Women Faculty in Science to all of my faculty colleagues. Please read it, contemplate its messages and information, and act upon it personally and collectively.
>
> I learned two particularly important lessons from this report and from discussions while it was being crafted. First, I have always believed that contemporary gender discrimination within universities is part reality and part perception. True, but I now understand that reality is by far the greater part of the balance. Second, I, like most of my male colleagues, believe that we are highly supportive of our junior women faculty members. This also is true. They generally are content and well supported in many, though not all dimensions. However, I sat bolt upright in my chair when a senior woman, who has felt unfairly treated for some time, said "I also felt very positive when I was young."

We can take pride in the candor of dialog that these women have brought to this issue and in the progress that we have made, but much remains to be done. Our remarkably diverse student body must be matched by an equally diverse faculty. Through our institutional commitment and policies we must redouble our efforts to make this a reality. (Vest 1999)

And substantial progress was made, though not without some push-back from MIT's male scientists and not without a little rancor in the end. A dozen years later, the *New York Times* summed up the experience, observing in the process what it called "Gains, and Drawbacks, for Female Professors."

While women on the tenure track 12 years ago feared that having a child would derail their careers, today's generous policies have made families the norm: the university provides a yearlong pause in the tenure clock, and everyone gets a term-long leave after the arrival of a child. There is day care on campus and subsidies for child care while traveling on business.

Yet now women say they are uneasy with the frequent invitations to appear on campus panels to discuss their work-life balance. In interviews for the study, they expressed frustration that parenthood remained a women's issue, rather than a family one. . . .

Administrators say some men use family leave to do outside work, instead of to be their children's primary care giver—creating more professional inequity.

And stereotypes remain: women must navigate a narrow "acceptable personality range," as one female professor said, that is "neither too aggressive nor too soft." Said another woman: "I am not patient and understanding. I'm busy and ambitious."

Despite an effort to educate colleagues about bias in letters of recommendation for tenure, those for men tend to focus on intellect while those for women dwell on temperament. (Zernicke 2011)

The last word belonged to Nancy Hopkins, who told the *Times*, "To women in my generation, these residual issues can sound small because we see so much progress. . . . But they're not small; they still create an unequal playing field for women—not just at universities, and certainly not just at M.I.T. And they're harder to change because they are a reflection of where women stand in society" (Zernicke 2011).

I draw two lessons from this story. The first is the singular importance of Charles Vest, not because he was a man but because he was the president, who could convene the necessary conversations and insist that they be focused on problem solving rather than problem broadcasting. The second lesson is that the fight is never over, no matter how we might wish that the personal discomfort and hurt feelings would go away.

Applying these lessons to problem-solving conversations about race is more than a little tricky. What I believe is needed is a deliberative discussion that seeks to make sense of the root causes of underrepresentation. The goal should be a renewed understanding of who isn't applying. Who isn't being admitted. Who isn't enrolling. Who isn't staying and why. And, the role that history has played in the maldistribution of opportunities will need to be a constant touchstone.

I remain leery of an open-ended exploration of the history of race relations in the nation as a whole. In the kind of problem-solving conversation I seek, there would be emotional moments to be sure, but hopefully the conversation would remain focused on practical solutions. These conversations are only possible if they are properly convened and initially given time to work through their tasks quietly, not in the dark, but out of the glare of a culture war that is threatening to engulf us all.

Lori: I agree that we need problem-solving conversations. One of those problems we face is that emotions and experience about difference haven't yet been processed sufficiently. Like nested dolls, there are conflicts within most conflicts. In personal relationships, sometimes we get stuck arguing about how we're arguing—or even what we're arguing about, right? Interpersonal communication scholars describe one such snag in conflict management as how we "punctuate the sequence." That is, getting to shared solutions is made more difficult when there are underlying differences in perceptions about when and how a situation began, in what order events unfolded, and whose version of that sequencing will prevail. We may also find destructive interaction patterns in that nest of conflicts; for example, in an intimate relationship when one partner routinely rushes to fix something (or even to shut down the interaction with a quick apology), the other can be disconfirmed, becoming convinced that his or her perspective has not been heard or acknowledged as real. "Minimizing, denying, and blaming" have their own slice on the classic power and control wheel—for good reason. Scholar and author Robin DiAngelo describes common behaviors that derail dialogues about race in workshops she leads, observing that among many white participants, "the smallest amount of racial stress is intolerable—the mere suggestion that being white has meaning often triggers a range of defensive responses. These include emotions such as anger, fear, and guilt and behaviors such as argumentation, silence, and withdrawal. . . . White fragility is not a weakness, per se. In fact, it is a powerful means [of] . . . control" (DiAngelo 2018).

One of the central problems impeding constructive conversations about race in higher education and elsewhere is that many who are white are especially resistant to engage in those dialogues. DiAngelo continues, un-nesting what initially may not be apparent, even to academics:

> Over time I began to see what lay beneath this anger and resistance to discuss race or listen to people of color. I began to see consistent responses from a variety of participants. For example, many white participants who lived in white suburban neighborhoods and had no sustained relationships with people of color were absolutely certain that they held no racial prejudice or animosity. Other participants simplistically reduced racism to a matter of nice people versus mean people. . . . There was both a knee jerk defensiveness about any suggestion that being white had meaning and a refusal to acknowledge any advantage to being white. . . . These responses were so predictable—so consistent and reliable—I was able to stop taking the resistance personally, get past my own conflict avoidance, and reflect on what was behind them. . . .
>
> I came to see that the way we are taught to define racism makes it virtually impossible for white people to understand it. Given our racial insulation, coupled with misinformation, any suggestion that we are

complicit in racism is a kind of unwelcome and insulting shock to the system.

If, however, I understand racism as a system into which I was socialized, I can receive feedback on my problematic racial patterns as a helpful way to support my learning and growth. (DiAngelo 2018)

Such a conclusion can be useful for discussions of gender as well, not removing responsibility but rather deepening understanding sufficiently so that a core component of the nested conflicts is explicitly addressed rather than obscured.

You have suggested that presidents need to use their leadership platform to convene these conversations. I agree and yet must surface another reality about how such a convening is framed. Because all of us in leadership roles have limitations to our lived histories, we must situate ourselves as regular listeners if we are to compel and enact change with both empathy and integrity.

In a research project on preaching, I asked clergy to listen to their listeners with a structured process as part of their weekly preaching preparation. At first, many of the clergy were sure they could facilitate open-ended conversations with their parishioners. It didn't work. Given their role in the congregation, clergy attempting to facilitate inevitably dominated the discussions instead, making definitive statements that shut down the sharing. Ultimately, the groups with external facilitators were much more functional, requiring clergy-leaders to quietly situate themselves as listeners. Symbolically and practically, the leader needed to communicate, "I still have a lot to learn, so I will keep listening before I attempt to make declarations from my pulpit." Importantly, when they were able to hold space to hear and integrate the perspectives of their listeners, the preachers—and their preaching—changed, in measurable ways. Said one, after hearing a listener's story of the abuse she experienced as a child, "What I planned to preach on the topic of forgiveness next week was a ridiculous oversimplification. I simply had no idea." I hear in that comment an echo of President Vest's revelation that he "sat bolt upright" in his chair when he listened deeply to the perspective of a female colleague at MIT.

DiAngelo reminds us, "If I am not aware of the barriers you face, then I won't see them much less be motivated to remove them" (DiAngelo 2018). While looking squarely in the face of the data is mandatory, looking squarely in one another's faces and listening deeply is also imperative. Rumbles about racism must deal with the layered conflicts, including the need for individual and collective awareness that comes from humbly listening to many points of view. And, decisions about the leadership and facilitation of these much-needed conversations are as critical as determining who will be in the room when it happens.

Right now, academic communities don't have either consensus about the process or progress on the problem. We need more than one kind of conversation to get us unmired from our perpetual paralysis.

Bob: I really don't want to disagree, though I do think you are not going to get to where you want to get. Not that the goal is wrong—it is both laudable and necessary. As a nation we do need a conversation focusing on cultural change. The problem is that there is no historical precedent for such a conversation taking place, let alone for changing how the nation sees itself or its constituent parts. To be sure, attitudes and perceptions of race and gender have changed, and for the most part for the better, but the process has taken decades. I think we need to change a lot faster than that. What I seek instead is a conversation about practicalities rather than cultural predilections, though I know the two are linked. What I am looking for is a conversation principally among campus leaders about how to go about changing the demography of the campus: more students of color, more graduating students of color, more faculty of color, and a curriculum that teaches about the richness of diversity without an unseemly focus on villains and victims. It would be a conversation that takes a tough look at the campuses' recruiting strategies and activities. A conversation that revisits what it means for a student to be college ready and a campus to be student ready. It would be a tough conversation, initially among the few rather than the many, about how to create a feeling of belonging across the campus and among all constituent groups. And it would be a conversation about practical things, things that can in fact be changed now. The result I believe would be a recasting of campus demographics and the creation of more welcoming communities.

I suspect it would be best if I stopped here, making my plea for practicality and then moving on. But I am really worried that we are heading in a wrong direction, one that is shaped, fueled really, by the anger of the advocates. The result is that a focus on cultural predilections will increasingly yield moments in time in which conversations about race and gender become weaponized. One such victim was Sarah Viren, a well-known scholar of the link between fiction and expository writing. The incident centered on a job search for which Viren had emerged as the leading candidate. She ended up turning down the offer and later reflected on her experience with a male competitor who had used the vagaries of the Title IX legislation to attack Viren's wife.

Viren told her story in a featured article in the *New York Times Magazine* with the title "The Accusations Were Lies. But Could We Prove It?" It is a tale that concludes with an observation highlighting the challenges we face as we seek collectively to redress past grievances.

> If I could return to that job interview from more than three years ago, to that moment when I was asked about my responsibility as a creative-nonfiction writer in the post-truth world, I know what I would say now: Our allegiance as nonfiction writers is not so much to truth as it is to honesty. Because truth can be spoken into a void, while honesty implies an audience, a reader, real people to whom you commit to tell your story as accurately and truthfully as you can so that they can then differentiate for themselves the facts from the lies, the truth from the fiction. (Viren 2020)

It's the audience that Viren speaks of that I think about often. Like you, I want us to speak to each other accurately and truthfully. And I am as well a skeptic. For example, I am not so sure that students of color are being turned away from our universities in the large numbers you are imagining, but I know they are choosing not to stay in large numbers. The retention numbers are truly alarming and deserve immediate remediation. We also need to address the question of why African American students choose to attend institutions that are fundamentally at risk in much larger numbers than any other group. But we should begin with the admissions quandary and the retention puzzle. Here, Beverly Tatum has made clear that in large part retention requires a true sense of belonging and that in turn requires the kind of understanding that you are urging on our readers. Ultimately the curriculum needs to be tackled, but that discussion becomes both easier and more productive the more representative our faculty and student bodies become. None of it is easy. All of it is necessary. And, if I can conclude with a plea for practically, all of it depends on getting started on changing the demographics—faculty as well as students—of our campuses now.

Lori: One of the hardest yet most central components of all the practical conversations we are attempting to incite is that as we have them, it becomes apparent that we in higher education are often part of the problem we want to solve. And I don't mean the rare but egregious misuse of policies meant to protect. I mean *most* of us. *Our* behaviors. *Our* attitudes. *Our* lack of awareness. *Our* silence. *Our* myopic focus. *Our* inertia. Becoming conscious of something can be the primary catalyst for changing it, but such broad and shared recognitions will only emerge if we commit to having the conversations in the first place. Thank you for being willing to rumble.

As individuals and a collective academic community, we are trained, enculturated really—to be The Experts, to solve the problems, and to provide The Answers. So, being vulnerable and situating ourselves as humble learners as opposed to experts is not something at which we may have had much practice. But we can do both—and these tough conversations about difference require us to engage differently, motivated by the compelling and complex nature of the problems and also by our connective tissue—a shared belief in the inherent value of learning. Yes, we must discern the facts from the fiction. Yes, leaders must charge action groups to review the realities and craft recommendations to transform practice at scale. And yes, too, that to do so will require us to embrace the discomfort of knowing that there is much *we* need to learn.

As we worked to complete this manuscript, we did so, like all of our conversation partners, from the confines of our homes as the COVID-19 pandemic raged. We've canceled trips that would allow the face-to-face interaction we treasure and have joined the world of Zoom—along with learners across all levels of education. At this moment of the global public health crisis, ambiguity is high, yet any attempt to model future higher education scenarios brings the intractable challenges of difference into sharp relief. On a day when manufacturers are rapidly changing production lines to fabricate personal protective equipment for healthcare workers and many people living in the United States have dramatically changed their behaviors to protect those among us who are most at risk, I find a mighty and realistic source of hope. We are showing ourselves to be capable of transformation for the purpose of collective good, and if that is true, nearly anything is possible.

As we know, there is no more difficult conversation to launch and sustain than one that focuses on race and gender. Freeman A. Hrabowski, long-serving president of the University of Maryland Baltimore County (UMBC) is among the handful of campus leaders who have succeeded in convening such conversations. As we set out to add our own voices to this effort, we began by consulting Freeman, who is both a friend and long-term collaborator. He warned us that it would not be easy and that we would likely discover as much about ourselves as about how cultural differences divide us. We then asked him to contribute his voice to our conversation, and he agreed. In the end, he asked two of his University of Maryland colleagues to join him, and thus the contribution below is jointly written by Freeman A. Hrabowski, J. Kathleen Tracy, and Peter H. Henderson. They join our conversation here.

Freeman A. Hrabowski, J. Kathleen Tracy, and Peter H. Henderson: We commend Lori and Bob for initiating a conversation about differences, and for agreeing and disagreeing with civility. Both have important perspectives to offer, even when discussing topics as challenging as race and gender in America. Our goal must be to deepen shared understanding through a discussion of history, data that illuminate current circumstances, and practical steps for addressing challenges and opportunities. How do we have the difficult conversations that can lead us to new understandings of these complex issues? We believe the keys are listening with civility and letting *evidence* guide our thinking about the path forward.

The three of us had a conversation of our own about the challenges of discussing race and gender. Since we bring different backgrounds, life experiences, and perspectives to this conversation—including race, gender, and sexual orientation—we thought to model the importance of hearing all voices by writing this piece together. Productive conversations emerge when those with different historical and personal experiences are included, when we take the time to listen to each other, and when we examine available data to establish a shared understanding of our challenges and opportunities.

We begin by acknowledging that change is possible. As we reflect on the past century, we find moments when attitudes have shifted concerning gender, race, and sexual orientation in America. Ratification of the 19th Amendment granting women's suffrage in 1920, landmark civil rights legislation in the 1960s, and the Supreme Court decision upholding same-sex marriage in 2015 all reflect progress on both personal and political levels. Similarly, the GI Bill, the Higher Education Act, and the Pell Grant program gave higher education tools to change who could go to and succeed in college, another profound shift in American culture and society.

Despite this progress, many Americans do not understand why race matters. As we write this, we are each working from home during the COVID-19 pandemic yet are engaged with the community about the management of the crisis. Recently, calls for our state government to provide case data by race/ethnicity in addition to county, age, and gender emerged. We joined others to argue that these data are essential for assessing disparate impact. Voices on social media, however, were quick to belittle this request, saying the "virus is not racist." In just the past few days as we write this, we are now seeing data from Milwaukee, Chicago, Louisiana, and nearby DC that show African Americans are more likely to be infected and die from coronavirus. To understand the disproportionate impact on our African American communities, we must be honest with ourselves about structural inequalities and health disparities that continue to exist and put communities at increased risk. We must use evidence to guide our actions.

After the tragic death of Freddie Gray, we at UMBC held a "teach-in" to ensure the campus had a shared understanding of the long history of racism in the Baltimore region. Faculty and staff gave talks about the history of redlining and racial residential segregation, cumulative disadvantage at the intersection of race and poverty, the educational and mental health needs of black Baltimoreans, and the importance of deeper conversations, engagement, and service with our community. Emerging from this difficult conversation about historical truths, many faculty—across all fields—said they wanted to lead conversations with their classes but needed training on how to do that in a way that was substantive, sensitive, and civil. We clearly needed to provide professional development for this, just as we do for faculty who redesign courses. The Faculty Development Center immediately developed a series of resources and campus consultations for "The Diverse Classroom," "Difficult Conversations," and "Crafting an Inclusive Course Climate."

Because of our success in broadening student access to higher education, universities are now a microcosm of our society. Yet, there is still work to be done to ensure that students of all backgrounds belong, participate, and succeed. The probability of a student from the lowest income group completing a bachelor's degree by age 24 is about 15 percent, not much higher than a half-century ago. As students of color are disproportionately represented in this group, again race and ethnicity matter. Our Meyerhoff Scholars program has demonstrated that we can support success of students from all backgrounds by setting high expectations, building community, promoting group work and experiential learning, and facilitating conversations about diversity, equity, and inclusion. We ensure that programs succeed by embedding evaluation into all of our student success initiatives.

There is also work to be done to ensure that faculty and administration more closely resemble the racial and gender diversity of our student populations. Despite advances, faculty remain overwhelmingly white, particularly in certain disciplines. Women and people of color continue to be underrepresented in leadership roles. The National Science Foundation's ADVANCE Program has provided a model for promoting the success of women faculty through new practices in recruiting, hiring, career advancement, and leadership development. At UMBC, we have also developed an initiative in which faculty counsel departments on how to undertake searches that produce broader, more diverse hiring pools and how to support new faculty with diverse backgrounds once they are on board. These initiatives require deep, trusting conversations.

Difficult conversations require us to "look in the mirror," tell the truth, and develop shared understanding of problems, evidence, and the range of possible solutions. At UMBC, our success in creating an empowered culture for conversations about differences starts with building trust and empathy, encouraging community members to be open-minded, and encouraging everyone to consider what it's like to walk in someone else's shoes. It also involves active listening and exploring and disaggregating data to a level of specificity that increases understanding. Finally, it's essential to develop allies and champions for the work. The leadership of the university's president and provost is necessary but not sufficient. What is critical for success is working with colleagues, including and especially faculty, to change the campus and the professoriate. Shared leadership is essential.

Lori: Since our conversation partners shared their perspectives, the pandemic has become ever more politicized and divisive—and the anguish of racial injustice has been further illuminated through tragedy. Some among us are despondent; others, simply exhausted. With this stark awareness, our call for campuses to host conversations about difference now becomes a plea. Where is a place devoted to evidence and human progress? Where is a community rich with diverse people capable of courageous leadership? Where too can we find those whose identities reflect a lifelong commitment to curiosity and learning? The core mission for institutions of higher education, our raison d'être, *compels us* to find a way to model truly democratic conversations that generate change. If we can engage in this discourse on difference—and we must—we will not only activate change within the academe; we will demonstrate anew our value to a society that sometimes wonders if we are still relevant. Bob's appeal for problem-based conversation that creates new solutions resonates well with the cry for action from the streets. Is there a way forward, a way out of the mess we're in? There is. Launch your campus conversations today. Pursue much needed connections. Listen to student voices and inspect evidence. Open the curriculum to "start-from-scratch" scrutiny. Look with clear eyes at financial realities and internal impediments. Find guidance in our conversation partners' principles, shared just above. Avoidance is no longer an option, and mere talk is cheap—but meaningful dialogues of difference will spur transformation.

Reflections

Our hope is that our conversations will convince you to join us in a genuine revitalization movement of a learning enterprise that is now too often disparaged. What we seek are conversations that use the transformative power of *learning* to assure for ourselves and our students lives well lived. Here we reflect on the nature of communicating, the practice of facilitating, and the "how to" of starting campus conversations.

The Soft Skill of the Century
Lori

Few would disagree that communicating is important. The term *communication* is everywhere. Embedded in lists of learning outcomes. Sprinkled through campus strategic plans. Identified as a required skill in position descriptions for nearly every higher education role. Deemed essential by employers that hire our alumni across all sectors. And most definitely used to describe what went wrong in all kinds of relationships and endeavors. Surely too, for each conversation topic in this book, less than perfect communication itself is often seen as the culprit. Higher education in a mess? Community missing on campus? Laden slogans stifling needed dialogue? Silos impervious to change? Faculty deemed irrelevant? Financial decisions not seeing the light of day? Committees dodging curricular downsizing? The achievement of equity proving elusive? Students not known or understood? Some—perhaps even you—might conclude that for all these higher education issues, the failure to communicate is at the root of the problem.

Yet we also exude ambivalence about the word, routinely describing communication as a "*soft* skill." With an eye roll, some who have heard the title of this book imagine the premise is simply to chat pleasantly until we have a grand kumbaya. How can communication be so central and yet also perceived as superficial? Why is it that we so often hear that the kinds of revitalizing conversations we seek require the rare commodity of trust, which not-so-incidentally is also produced or eroded through communication? How can Brené Brown's challenge to "rumble" be so difficult if it's all so simple?

Just now, my Google search for *communication* yielded 4,030,000,000 options in 0.48 seconds. A quick perusal of the first few sites yielded lots of "tips and tricks" for getting your way in conversations, improving relationships, and managing the fear of public speaking. A move to "Google Scholar" diminished the number of listed sites to 6,710,000. Most of those results are published in journals of the National Communication Association (NCA), a vibrant professional organization that connects a vast array of scholars. The NCA website describes communication as "the discipline that studies all forms, modes, media, and consequences of communication through humanistic, social scientific, and aesthetic inquiry" (NCA 2020). While the scholarship of this discipline spans a wide range of specialties, Bob and I are specifically focused on interpersonal and small group interaction, commonly known as conversation. Within that frame of scholarly focus, you can find theory, discourse analysis, and reams of research results relevant to the premise of this book. And yet, with all the public interest in communication and all this scholarship, we still are stymied by some basics—like conversing in ways that build trust across cultures and roles—and engaging in ethical persuasion that leads to systemic change. What's so hard about this soft skill?

Remember Robert Kegan and Lisa Lahey, the Harvard organizational psychologists we drew on for our conversation about the slogans that ensnare? They contend that if we want to change and we aren't changing, we must uncover our competing commitments and big assumptions—and then take action to challenge both. In the original *Harvard Business Review* article, "The Real Reason People Won't Change" (2001), which developed into the book *Immunity to Change: How to Overcome It and Unlock the Potential in Yourself and Your Organization* (2009), they ask us to ask ourselves, "What are you doing, or not doing, that is keeping your commitment from being more fully realized?" If you're among those of us committed to revitalizing higher education, a good rumble with your assumptions about human communication is in order. Again, Kegan and Lahey implore, "Only by bringing big assumptions to light can people . . . recognize why they are engaging in seemingly contradictory behavior" (Kegan and Lahey 2001).

One of those major assumptions is that communication is mere "message sending." The image of a model more relevant for machines than people may be unconsciously contaminating your thinking about the process of human communication. That "Shannon-Weaver Mathematical Model of Communication" published in a Bell Laboratories technical journal in 1948 shows straight arrows moving in one direction, includes nouns like *sender* and *receiver*, and refers to the misleading verb *transmit*. Communication theorists have crafted many new depictions of the process since then, but it doesn't take an expert to realize the widely known model is insufficient. Life has shown us that we aren't tossing little messages back and forth—either catching or dropping them—nor are we educators opening up students' heads to pour in edifying content. Something much more complex is occurring as we think and act and talk, struggling together to construct shared meaning, informed by the context (including previous conversations). Leaving this underlying "information transmission" assumption uninspected may lead us to believe our words have been "received" or worse yet, that if the "receivers" didn't get the message as we intended, they are to blame. The vestiges of that way of thinking about communication led to other counterproductive assumptions as well, like imagining that if we senders are clear and well-intentioned, we are effective. The conversational style of this book was designed to contrast with the typical one-way transmission assumption of many volumes— expert authors telling a presumably receptive reader what they know. Instead, we sought to model how conversation shifts thinking and generates new ideas for action.

As we inspect our assumptions about communication, we are moved to a more complex understanding of what's happening when we talk to each other. After all, the kinds of creative yet inherently conflictual conversations we seek are those that will change minds and inspire new types of action. That's possible because speech and thought intertwine in a complex and dynamic process. The translation of Russian philosopher L. S. Vygotsky's collected works begins with the premise that to study speech and thought separately in an effort to understand human communication would be akin to studying hydrogen and oxygen separately to try to understand water (Rieber and Carton 1987). To skip the philosophical and get right to the practical, think through the nuances of a recent argument (and the follow-up dispute about who said what, how they said it, and what they really meant). Think too about how to converse with both candor and empathy. To be clear while also demonstrating cultural humility. To advocate while also listening, modifying your words to integrate what you've just heard. To change one's mind midsentence, as the process of speaking clarifies your thought. To deepen a relationship through the vulnerability of self-disclosure, tuned to nuances of the response. To apologize and make lasting amends. To learn while teaching.

Human communication serves much more substantive functions than the transmission of information: *it clarifies and shapes thought, connects people and ideas, and provides the opportunity for influence, learning, and even change.*

As an educator, I find these functions of human communication exceptionally motivating and grounding. I just left a Zoom meeting with other college leaders. We talked about the murder of George Floyd. We talked about COVID-19. We talked about the flooded campus of one among us. We imagined the upcoming historic semester, with a presidential election and anticipated physical distance. An eavesdropper might conclude that we were just saying stuff to each other—that nothing happened, no votes, no decisions, nothing. They would be wrong. Thoughts shifted. Relationships deepened. Seeds were planted. In subtle ways, we are thinking differently because we talked.

Conversation is an inherently powerful mechanism of transformation, one of the primary catalysts for individual and collective learning. I live with keen awareness and deep responsibility, knowing that every spoken word, every interaction, holds the potential for lasting impact. And while many words evaporate, others live on. I'm guessing that right now, with only a brief pause, you can bring to mind pivotal conversations that caused years of pain and others that opened new possibilities you hadn't yet imagined. Yes? While human communication can be used for great evil or great good, it is most often squandered in mediocrity.

As you've been inspecting your assumptions about the nature of communication, you may also have discerned some of the countercommitments that are impeding progress. Why haven't we yet used conversation to transform higher education? Perhaps we're more committed to being right, to avoiding direct confrontation, to protecting our power, to believing that things can't change, to preserving the way things are so the value of our work can't be questioned, or to staying safe and comfortable. Perhaps to strengthen communication we must relax these countercommitments and in so doing, soften ourselves and the blockade that protects not only our personal interaction habits but also higher ed's way of being. What if we were committed instead to approaching conversations with humility, recognizing we have as much to learn as we have to share? What if we lowered our defenses to enter these deliberate dialogues committed to the notion that there is more to discover about ourselves and the way higher education works? What if we accepted that if higher education is to innovate and adapt, we personally will have to do things differently? What if we began by seeking out these conversations and elevating our expectations for what can happen as we engage with each other?

In his famous work, *I and Thou* (1923), philosopher Martin Buber developed his central thesis, that it is only through dialogue that we become fully human. That kind of conversation is a rumble that requires courage. That kind of conversation has the potential to transform higher education. And that kind of sustained conversation demands something different in our habits of interaction—expressing genuine thought and emotion, actively recognizing the worth of the other in how and what is said, conveying and affirming a spirit of equality, and developing a supportive, trusting climate. Those soft yet significant conditions are established through conversation, and they amplify the potential power of those conversations as well.

What's next? Will higher education *as it is* still propel learning in an age characterized by the exponential acceleration of artificial intelligence? Can something as soft as human communication even matter in such a future? In the introduction to his 2020 book, *Teaching Values of Being Human: A Curriculum That Links Education, the Mind and the Heart*, Mark Le Messurier writes: "When all is said and done, AI will never usurp our humanness. It is the human qualities we must highlight, teach, and develop . . . because the jobs likely to be future-proofed are those that radiate human qualities of understanding, connections and collaborative skills at peak levels" (Le Messurier, 2020). So, yes, while machines are getting better and better at being machines, we can complement that rapid change by getting better and better at being human. We humans have a distinctive and underutilized capacity for transformative communication, one that needs acceleration if we are to shape our own future.

The Art of Facilitation
Bob

Teaching remotely this past spring has taught many lessons, most of them new, but a few older and deserving of renewed attention. Two weeks into my program's switch from in-person to remote classes, we convened a Zoom session to calibrate what was and wasn't working. To a person my colleagues reported they could not begin class as they had planned—as they had when everyone was in the same space. Turned out the students wanted to talk with each other, catch-up on what living and working in isolation was like. Only when they were ready could my colleagues begin the PowerPoint demos and exercises they had so carefully planned.

I was the only one on Zoom that afternoon who reported I could begin my class as I had every session for the past year—by asking, "What's on your mind?" It was an exercise that had become a habit of mind, something the students came to class prepared to do whether in person or in the Zoom zone. The idea for the exercise had come from James Zull's *The Art of Changing the Brain: Enriching the Practice of Teaching by Exploring the Biology of Learning,* first published in 2002. It is a volume that succeeded wildly in introducing its readers to what the neurosciences could teach us about the learning processes of our students (and ourselves). Zull was not himself a neuroscientist but rather a professor of biology and biochemistry whose lot in life was often the teaching of Case Western Reserve's large contingent of freshmen pre-meds. At some point his curiosity led him to ask his colleagues in the neurosciences to teach him what they were learning about the brain. And then he set out to teach us, not as a researcher but as an explainer and facilitator.

Zull teaches two important lessons. First, that learning is not metaphorical but physical. Learning quite literally changes the brain. The neurosciences were mapping where and when learning happened and where we stored what we came to know. Learning is a process remarkably similar to the kind of process Lori describes as integral to communication. It is one of the reasons she is so insistent that those committed to teaching need to take a "deep dive" in the literature of the neurosciences in order to have a grounded understanding of what we ought to be doing and the learning processes we need to promote.

The second lesson Zull teaches is that learning is a storage process—and, as in all good storage systems, there need to be protocols for de-accessing information as well as acquiring it. Here Zull is at his practical best. What alarms him is the professoriate's penchant for telling their classes "to forget everything you think you know about our subject. I am going to supply you with the correct answers." Learning doesn't work that way—we can't simply erase bad information; we must first go through a process of substituting the good for wrong. And that process begins, not with the teacher broadcasting truth but with the learners accessing what they already know or think they know. Hence the importance of asking "what's on your mind?" as a way for cuing learners that the process begins with them.

I have started my comments on the nature and importance of facilitation here because facilitating is a process closely akin to the process of teaching—the same rules and protocols apply. Nothing is straightforward; almost all successfully facilitated conversations are circular, in and out, back and forth. It's one of the reasons facilitated conversations take so much time. And why the success of the conversation directly depends on the skill of the facilitator to move the conversation forward, stirring the pot when necessary and letting the conversation drift as the participants explore what they know and don't know and what they are prepared to learn either now or later.

One of the secrets to a successfully facilitated conversation is an abundance of stories. It helps if the facilitator her or himself is a natural storyteller and has done the necessary homework ahead of time to know the kind of stories that are—and are not—likely to enrich the conversation. Just as important is the skill to draw on the stories the participants tell to reinforce the group's ability to draw conclusions and imagine concrete examples. My most vivid illustration of this aspect of facilitation comes from my working with a Pew-sponsored roundtable convened by the University of Montana. It was a tough time for the school, as the political coalition most hostile to the university had secured an enhanced majority in the Montana House of Representatives. As the discussion drifted into unfriendly territory, I looked across the table to a senior member of the faculty who was visibly distressed. I have a rule that whenever a member of the group shows physically that they are either unhappy or unnerved by the group's conversation, I call on that person, which I did on this occasion. Between clenched teeth—literally—she spit back at me, "Well he is a sonofabitch, but he is our sonofabitch." I was at loss as to where to go next until the president of the university rescued me by noting that the sonofabitch she had in mind was the new Speaker of the House of Representatives, who, while at the university, had been her star pupil. The ice was broken. Thereafter, whenever a sticky wicket was encountered, it was to be discussed in terms of each narrative's responsible "sonofabitch."

I offer this story as a means of making several points about good facilitation. Beyond stories, it helps if the facilitator can extract personal narratives from the participants—the kind that can provide a cloak of verisimilitude to the arguments each participant wants to make. Often it will be up to the facilitator to make explicit the lessons a particular story teaches, and more generally it is the facilitator who must regularly sum up the discussion to date. Above all, the facilitator must know in advance the range and scope of the opinions likely to be expressed—in a word, facilitators need to do their homework.

To the extent possible, I try to talk individually with each of the participants of a discussion I am expected to facilitate. Everybody has his or her own "signature," what gamblers call a *tell*. The more the facilitator knows about these individual signs, the better. What also works is to have someone closely associated with the facilitator interview each participant in advance and then brief the facilitator on the collective nature of the group. Such interviews often help to identify in advance the stories and parables individual participants might be ready to contribute once the group's discussion is under way.

Good facilitated discussions do not go on forever. I have found a three-hour block to be a manageable length—and I don't take breaks during the session, telling participants to leave the session when necessary and then be sure to return. When asked why, I simply observe that it is hard enough to get a good discussion started without having to worry about restarting it.

The Pew Roundtable process I described in our opening conversation involved a more elaborate process. The maximum number of participants was set at 30. Roundtables with fewer than 15 participants often yielded awkward discussions. We would open with a dinner session of three hours to be followed by two three-hour blocks the next day. We repeatedly found the sessions that included food were more productive, often because they were both more civil and congenial. In addition to the facilitator, there was an extra staff member who served as the roundtable's scribe, responsible for taking the notes that were next converted into a 10-page or so thought paper coauthored by the facilitator and scribe and signed off by the convener of the roundtable. For most of the roundtables I facilitated, the scribe was Greg Wegner, who has played an important role in preparing the manuscript for this publication. Greg is a scholar with an unbelievable capacity for listening to the rhythms of speech and argument. A holder of a PhD in English from Penn, Greg is a gifted writer in his own right. Currently he serves as the director of program development at the Great Lakes Colleges Association.

One final thought. I am often asked whether the president of the institution might serve as the facilitator. My answer is an emphatic no. Though most presidents have the skills to facilitate, they can't achieve the necessary neutrality on their own campus. What they have to say matters mightily, and they are expected to speak out whenever they are in attendance. But they can't be expected to voice both sides of each argument, as a good facilitator must always do.

Getting Campus Conversations Started
Lori and Bob

What concludes our volume is practical guidance for those new to convening and facilitating transformative dialogue. Such communication strategies are the starting place for change, acknowledging the power of human communication to clarify thought, connect people and ideas, and provide the opportunity for persuasion—depending on the skill of the facilitator.

Any campus citizen can convene conversations, so don't feel limited by your role—whatever it may be. Perhaps your teaching and learning center, equity office, or some other entity already has periodic organized dialogues. If so, you could propose to use the first five topics in this book for a set of sessions that are part of an established endeavor. If not, you could consider organizing a book club, a professional development seminar, a standing agenda item for an ongoing meeting, or even an online chat group. What's ideal is for you to invite individuals from a wide array of roles and contexts within your campus community: for example, faculty from varied disciplines and colleges, student development personnel, a recruiter or alumni relations staff member, an administrative leader (if you can bear it), and a few students with differing backgrounds. The more diversity, the richer the conversation.

Numbers matter. For these initial conversations, no fewer than 5, no greater than 12. If you are fortunate to have great interest in your campus conversation, up to 30 respondents could be divided into multiple groups that conclude in a joint meet-up. Even more ideal? Have food and beverages available and gather in a comfortable location, away from anyone's academic home base. If you're fortunate enough to know a great facilitator who is available, invite that person to participate. Otherwise, designate a participant to play the facilitation role for each conversation. Craft open-ended prompts and questions to launch, and guide each dialogue. These launching questions are embedded within each conversation, though you may wish to frame them more specifically for your campus context. Some practicalities are vital for sustaining the conversation endeavor: Stick to the time limit you establish at each gathering. Set up some basic expectations for the participants and the process: *Read the chapter in advance. Come prepared to share stories or perspectives from your experience. Be ready to listen. Keep what is shared confidential unless specific permission for broader sharing is granted. Stay open to what emerges from the group's interaction. Show respect when you disagree. Ask open-ended questions. Probe assumptions, tracking the group's need for data or evidence.*

It is likely that given recent events, campus leaders will be creating and empowering rapid response teams, with deadlines to produce action recommendations on two of the topics we address in the latter part of this book: money and difference. We urge these campus leaders to insist that robust conversation about the curriculum and students be embedded in the charges to groups creating financial and equity recommendations. The grief, anguish, and anger experienced during the pandemic and the protests against racial injustice in 2020 are serving as a disruption in all sectors, including higher education.

This leadership moment is historic. Declarations and mandates aren't enough to propel the reengineering or revitalization of higher education. Deep, rich, real rumbles can be designed to activate transformation, sustaining higher education's essential place in society. We must engage. We must learn about ourselves. We must adapt. The time is now.

Time to Take the Plunge

Now it is your turn. Without conversations there will not be change. Without testifiers and provocateurs there will be no talk that's worth the walk. We conclude by offering an even dozen of what we call conversation starters.

1. When you open your eyes, what do you see out there?
2. Which lens or perspective of higher education is most challenging to comprehend and appreciate; that is, with whom do you most need to talk?
3. What activities hold the potential to increase connectedness among our faculty? Among our students? Among all in our community?
4. How might we lower costs in the short run? In the long run?
5. What are the competencies we need to teach our students to succeed in today's economy? To contribute to solutions to today's societal challenges?
6. What is the biggest change to our curriculum that you can imagine?
7. What practical steps can we take to increase black, indigenous, and people of color among our faculty? Our students?
8. What big assumptions do we hold about the current and future states of American higher education?
9. What are we learning in higher education right now? What should we change first?

10. What communication habits impede our progress? What new habits could we cultivate to accelerate transformation?
11. How do the mechanisms for enacting change on our campus need to change?
12. What's on your mind?

So—go get started! You have nothing to lose except the possibility of using this moment to spark the revitalization of American higher education.

Bain, Ken. 2004. *What the Best College Teachers Do*. Cambridge, MA: Harvard University Press.

Bass, Randall. 2012. "Disrupting Ourselves: The Problem of Learning in Higher Education." March 21. *Educause Review*. https://er.educause.edu/articles /2012/3/disrupting-ourselves-the-problem-of-learning-in-higher-education.

Bok, Derek. 2017. *The Struggle to Reform Our Colleges*. Princeton, NJ: Princeton University Press.

Bowen, Howard R. 1980. *The Costs of Higher Education: How Much Do Colleges and Universities Spend per Student and How Much Should They Spend?* New York: Carnegie Council.

Brown, Brené. 2018. *Dare to Lead: Brave Work, Tough Conversations, Whole Hearts*. New York: Random House.

Buber, Martin. 1923. *I and Thou*. Translated by Walter Kaufmann. New York: Charles Scribner's Sons, 1970.

Chavis, David M., and Kien Lee. 2015. "What Is Community Anyway?" *Stanford Social Innovation Review*. May 12. https://ssir.org/articles/entry/what_is _community_anyway.

Davidson, Cathy. 2017. *The New Education: How to Revolutionize the University to Prepare Students for a World in Flux*. New York: Basic Books.

DiAngelo, Robin. 2018. *White Fragility: Why It's So Hard for White People to Talk about Racism*. Boston: Beacon Press.

Dimock, Michael. 2019. "An Update on Our Research into Trust, Facts and Democracy." Pew Research Center, June 5. https://www.pewresearch.org /2019/06/05/an-update-on-our-research-into-trust-facts-and-democracy.

Flanagan, Peggy. 2019. Inaugural Address. MPR News, January 10. https:// www.youtube.com/watch?v=wCAsi7vjEWg.

Frost, Robert. 1916. "The Road Not Taken." In *Mountain Interval*. New York: Henry Holt.

Gawande, Atul. 2017. *Being Mortal: Medicine and What Matters in the End*. New York: Henry Holt.

Georgetown University. "Core Pathways." Accessed May 23, 2020. https:// corepathways.georgetown.edu.

———. "Introducing the Red House at Georgetown." Accessed May 23, 2020. https://futures.georgetown.edu/introducing-the-red-house-at-georgetown.

Huber, Mary Taylor. 2019. "What Does Higher Education Need: Revolution and/or Reform?" *Change: The Magazine of Higher Learning*, March 26. https://www.tandfonline.com/doi/full/10.1080/00091383.2019.1569969.

Kegan, Robert, and Lisa Laskow Lahey. 2001. "The Real Reason People Won't Change." *Harvard Business Review*, November. http://ceewl.ca/12599-PDF-ENG.PDF#page=78.

———. 2009. *Immunity to Change: How to Overcome It and Unlock the Potential in Yourself and Your Organization.* Boston: Harvard Business School Publishing Corp.

Kendi, Ibram X. 2019. *How to Be an Antiracist.* New York: Penguin Random House.

Le Messurier, Mark. 2020. *Teaching Values of Being Human: A Curriculum That Links Education, the Mind and the Heart.* New York: Routledge.

Light, Kate. 2003. "There Comes the Strangest Moment." In *Open Slowly.* Lincoln, NE: Zoo Press.

Lukianoff, Greg, and Jonathan Haidt. 2018. *The Coddling of the American Mind: How Good Intentions and Bad Ideas Are Setting Up a Generation for Failure.* New York: Penguin Press.

Martin, Roger H. 2010. *Racing Odysseus: A College President Becomes a Freshman Again.* Berkeley: University of California Press.

Massy, William F. 2020. *Resource Management for Colleges and Universities.* Baltimore, MD: Johns Hopkins University Press.

NCA (National Communication Association). 2020. May 31. https://www.natcom.org.

Nelson, Trisalyn, and Jessica Early. 2020. "How to Counter the Isolation of Academic Life." *Chronicle of Higher Education*, February 2. https://www.chronicle.com/article/how-to-counter-the-isolation-of-academic-life/?cid2=gen_login_refresh&cid=gen_sign_in.

Nichols, Laura. 2020a. *The Journey before Us: First-Generation Pathways from Middle School to College.* New Brunswick, NJ: Rutgers University Press.

———. 2020b. "The Journey before Us." Interview by Scott Jaschik. *Inside Higher Ed*, January 15. https://www.insidehighered.com/news/2020/01/15/author-discusses-her-new-book-first-generation-students.

Reddit. 2020. https://www.reddit.com/r/highereducation.

Rieber, Robert W., and Aaron S. Carton, eds. 1987. *The Collected Works of L. S. Vygotsky.* New York: Plenum Press.

Rogers, Everett M. 1962/2003. *Diffusion of Innovations.* 5th ed. New York: Free Press.

Van Oot, Torey. 2020. "Minnesota Business Leaders Launch Push for Constitutional Amendment on Education." *Minneapolis Star Tribune*, February 11. https://www.startribune.com/minnesota-business-leaders-push-for-education-reform/567749312.

Vest, Charles M. 1999. "Introductory Comments." In *A Study on the Status of Women Faculty in Science.* Cambridge, MA: MIT.

Viren, Sarah. 2020. "The Accusations Were Lies. But Could We Prove It?" *New York Times Magazine*, March 18.

Wallace, Anthony F. C. 1956. "Revitalization Movements." *American Anthropologist*, n.s., 58, no. 2 (April): 264–81.

———. 1966. *Religion: An Anthropological View.* New York: Random House.

Walz, Tim. 2019. Inaugural Address. MPR News, January 10. https://www.youtube.com/watch?v=wCAsi7vjEWg.

Walzer, Norman, and Liz Weaver, eds. 2019. *Using Collective Impact to Bring Community Change.* New York: Routledge.

Watzlawick, Paul. 1976. *How Real Is Real? Confusion, Disinformation, Communication.* New York: Random House.

Westover, Tara. 2019. Keynote Address. American Council on Education, 101st annual meeting, Philadelphia.

Zemsky, Robert, Susan Shaman, and Susan Campbell Baldridge. 2020. *The College Stress Test: Tracking Institutional Futures across a Crowded Market.* Baltimore, MD: Johns Hopkins University Press.

Zemsky, Robert, Gregory R. Wegner, and Ann J. Duffield. 2018. *Making Sense of the College Curriculum: Faculty Stories of Change, Conflict, and Accommodation.* New Brunswick, NJ: Rutgers University Press.

Zernicke, Kate. 2011. "Gains, and Drawbacks, for Female Professors." *New York Times*, May 21.

Zull, James E. 2002. *The Art of Changing the Brain: Enriching the Practice of Teaching by Exploring the Biology of Learning.* Sterling, VA: Stylus Publishing.